ASHWELL

Village life in war and peace
1939-1975

Norman Gurney and Albert Sheldrick

Cortney Publications Ashwell

DEDICATION

This book is dedicated
to those who served their
King, Country and Village in
War so that we might
live in peace.

ISBN 0 904378 41 1

Published by Cortney Publications,
57 Ashwell Street, Ashwell, Baldock, Herts.

Cover design by Colin Barker (Whaddon)
Word processing by Judith Catterick (Ashwell)
Page preparation by Word Design Technology (Clifton)
Reproduction film by Monographics (Dunstable)
Printing and Binding by
Woolnough Bookbinding Ltd. (Irthlingborough)

Contents

Authorship: On some of the headings the author is indicated by the initials NJG or AS, all other parts have been written jointly.

Photographs: Credit to the donor is normally given at the end of each caption, in brackets, and if the photographer is known, the name is shown before the donor i.e. (Philip Coverdale/Museum)

Acknowledgements

We are deeply appreciative of the help we have received in preparing this book. A great deal of research has been involved and so many have helped us to find the answers to our many questions.

We must particularly thank Olive Anderson for her documentation of the Festival; Philip Crump and Bessie Wallace for their continuous and patient help and advice; Anthony Catterick for his invaluable collection of information and photographs of the Catterick era; Peter Howes and Byron Searle whose wide knowledge of Ashwell in the post-war period has been tremendously useful; Margaret Langley (nee Bulley), Leo Pickett, Marie and Pauline Whitby for their reminiscences and especially the chapter by Pauline on Ashwell's theatrical record. Roy York an evacuee to the village in the war also provided some very interesting reminiscences. Drs John and Sheila Moynihan contributed a great deal to the chapter on Ashwell's doctors, and Alan Picking's information and photographs connected with the war and the school here, enriched the book. We were entranced by Ethel Dilley's reminiscences and Terry Knight of Hitchin contributed two unusual labelled bottles of Christy's minerals and Page's Pale Ale which we have had photographed, plus a rare photograph of Russell's the Chemists.

We are grateful to Eric Gurney and Roy Jarman, Roy Holloway and Sam Wallace for their help on the farming section; George Berry on the Home Guard, the Engine Flower Show and the Senior Citizens Club; his wife Dorothy on the Fordham era; Hannah and Howard Day for information about the Bakery etc; Albert Bush, Kathleen Mack and Nan Gerard for facts about the Bank Holiday Show; Robin Dunlop's assistance regarding church finances and the Housing Association, Sue Harris on the Ashwell Association and David Short for advice on various matters.

We received a variety of information and/or photographs from Dorothy Andrews, Joyce Andrews, Adam Barr, Roy Bonnett, Mollie Bryant, Peter Bryant, Mrs Bullard (Senior), her daughter Phyllis Webster, Harry and Audrey Bullard, John and Joyce Collins, Anne and Lindsay Colquhoun, Geoff and May Cook, Philip Coverdale, Colin Crocker, Nancy Eversden, Mavis Fox, Marjorie Gentle, Mary Haylock, Mrs Izzard, Cliff Jenkinson, Arthur Kirchin, Betty and Rene Lawrence, Mrs L. MacBeth, Ross Moynihan, Rev. Frank Pickard, John Pollock, Mary Radford, Stan Raven, Nora Reeves, Dorothy Roberts, Betty Rogers, Robert Sheldrick, Doris Shelton, Gurney Sheppard, Mr and Mrs Jim Smith, Mrs Nancy Simmons, Pat Thorpe, Ken Wells, Gwenda and John Westrope, Andrew Whitehead, Pearl Williams, Joan Wilson, Theo Worboys and Ian Wright.

The wide range of photographs owes a great deal to those who have taken the trouble to lend them, but especially to the Ashwell Museum's collection. It has also been of the greatest value to be able to work in the Museum – our warm thanks to Peter Greener. Our researches have benefited from information gathered from the County Record Office at Hertford; the Museums at Hitchin and Letchworth; the Diocesan Offices at St Albans and Peterborough; the Minutes and Records of various organisations, which include Ashwell Parish Council, Women's Institute, the Ashwell branch of the Royal British Legion, Parochial Church Council, United Reformed Church, Infant Welfare, the Ashwell Association, Ashwell Housing Association, Senior Citizen's Club and Horticultural Society. We have been able to include extracts or photographs from various newspapers, which are appropriately acknowledged where they appear. We are particularly grateful to Aerofilms of Borehamwood for permission to use aerial photographs of Ashwell – photographs from their comprehensive collection are available at special prices.

Albert Sheldrick would like to thank Harold Briercliffe and Arthur Schofield for their editorial work.

If we have omitted anyone from the above, please accept our apologies and our appreciation. Let us know also if you spot any errors — we will correct them in any further editions.

Cortney Publications

Introduction

When we published "A Different World – Ashwell before 1939" we had no thought of a sequel. Its subsequent success and Albert's researches into the Second World War prompted various people to suggest that another book would be welcomed. This has certainly been confirmed by the pre-publication orders we have received, and for which we are most encouraged.

Why should Ashwell deserve such attention? Its population was not much more than it was in 1881 when it was 1,568; a hundred years later it was 1,617. It dipped in between to 1,132 in 1931. Most of us are glad that it has retained its compactness; renovation and restoration of the old rather than demolition and high density development has been the order of the day. But one of the reasons we finished our narrative at 1975 is that by then the major housing estates had either been built or their development agreed. Thereafter infilling in a fairly restricted sort of way was the rule. The composition of the Council also was in for change – five of the post war Councillors resigned in 1975.

But Ashwell while rich in tradition and history has had to come to terms with big changes. There is hardly a single facet of life which has not been affected – education, health, transport, work, shopping and leisure. Above all, the war has been the biggest engine of change. Television, in 1939 a rarity became commonplace by 1975. Fortunately while some of the old institutions have disappeared others have taken their place. The newcomers who came to Ashwell, many living in the new estates, have had an invigorating influence. Their assimilation has not always been easy – we have many families who go back for many generations. Of those who had attended the Primary School and were present at the Centenary Celebrations in 1978, 60 per cent were still living in the village. So the old and the new have needed time to get used to each other. It has been a fascinating task to research the years between 1939 and 1975. The wealth of material has been staggering. We have had to leave out much that we would like to have included.

But we hope you will find it a treasury of information spiced with anecdotes and humour, with a wonderful range and variety of photographs. And like its predecessor we hope it will travel to all four corners of the world.

We would like to express our warm appreciation to Judith Catterick and David Brundle (of Word Design Technology) both for their willingness to work all hours and technical expertise; to Monographics for the quality and speed of their reprographic service; to Norman's daughter Rachel Gurney-Crabtree for her skilful administrative assistance; and to both wives for their patience and help in a variety of ways.

Norman J. Gurney

Albert W. Sheldrick

An aerial view of Ashwell in the 1960's. (Aerofilms Ltd)

Ashwell at War 1939-45 (AS)

The approach of war

'Indeed I think that people want peace so much that one of these days governments had better get out of their way and let them have it.' These were the brave words of Dwight D. Eisenhower, one time President of the United States of America and formerly the Supreme Commander of the Allied forces during World War II.

At least half a dozen Ashwell men fought in the Boer War. Then just as the village had settled down again, army manoeuvres were held around Ashwell during the summer of 1914 and on one Sunday in July the villagers were entertained by the pipes of the Seaforth Highlanders when they and the Irish Fusiliers marched through the village, after watering their horses at the springs. The people of Ashwell were sad when they heard later that both regiments were wiped out at the first battle of the Somme.

So from August 1914 to November 1918 Ashwell was involved in what was known as the 'Great War', which was said to be the war to end all wars. Edward Snow Fordham, of Elbrook House, offered a gold sovereign to each Ashwell man who volunteered for the services. Some 250 men either volunteered or were conscripted into the Army, Navy and Royal Flying Corps. Forty-two failed to return.

With the war ending, the signing of the Treaty of Versailles, and the occupation of Germany by the Allies, the body of an unknown soldier was buried in Westminster Abbey, a national day of remembrance was ordered and at the stroke of the eleventh hour of the eleventh day of the eleventh month of each year the country came to a standstill, traffic halted and we all stopped whatever we were doing for two minutes. For we young ones it was to remember fathers, uncles or cousins, for those who had fought to remember brothers, friends or comrades. Grannie Sheldrick, with a tear in her eye, often looked across the room at the photographs of her two sons John and Bertie, both of whom were killed. All over the country memorials were erected in memory of 'Our glorious dead'. I remember wherever we were working on Armistice day, builder Fred Bray would look at his watch, a gold half hunter, and at 11 o'clock, with a serious look on his face, would say, 'It's eleven o'clock, chaps'. Ex-servicemen Jimmy Taylor and Alec Badcock, from Litlington, would lay down their trowels, Bill Waldock would stick his shovel into a heap of mortar and take the clay pipe out of his mouth. Bill had not only served in France but as a young soldier had seen service in India, while Charley Smith, a Radwell carpenter, laid down his saw. Some time afterwards we discovered that he had been thinking of the French girl he had left behind. Many, many years later, after the death of her husband, she brought over her two daughters and married Charles, who had remained a bachelor. During the year 1938 I was asked to visit Mr W A Appleton, CBE, JP, at his home, Townsend Close. Mr Appleton went to great lengths to explain to me that we were on the verge of a terrible war, the like of which had never been seen before and in which the whole world would be involved. He went on to tell me that as a young man he was Secretary to one of the British delegations at the Armistice conference held at Versailles just after the Great War, to sort out the vast problems and to ensure that war never happened again. "But", said Mr Appleton, "the Presidents and Prime Ministers of the countries involved spent more time socialising with their wives at the great dinners and splendid balls than they did on the boundaries and problems of the post-war Europe." In his opinion, they were partly to blame for the coming war.

An article appeared in the monthly Toc H journal at about the same time, pointing out the evils of National Socialism and giving a set of maps actually showing the order in which Hitler intended to take over the countries of Europe.

War declared

On the morning of Sunday, 3 September, 1939 Prime Minister, Neville Chamberlain, broadcast to the nation, saying, "We are at war with Germany". As the broadcast ended, the air raid sirens wailed throughout the land, a grim warning of what was to come. A year earlier, Navy, Army and Air Force reservists had been recalled and kitted out ready for an emergency.

Joe West, my wife's brother, had become a volunteer fireman with the West Ham Fire Service in 1938. Towards the end of August, 1939, Joe was instructed to report for full-time duty on 1 September. So on that morning Joe brought Dolly, his wife, and Josie, their baby daughter, to stay with us, then he returned to become a full-time fireman, knowing that that was the end of his shoe-repair business.

Joe was involved in some of the worst fires during the blitz on London. Dolly, in the meantime, found a cottage to rent and Joe was able, on his occasional day off duty, to come down to Ashwell. He was with the West Ham Fire Service until the war ended, when the National Fire Service was disbanded. He then decided to stay and work in Ashwell.

On Friday, 1 September, 1939, trainloads of school children, escorted by teachers and helpers, had left London for the safety of country towns and villages. One such trainload from Christchurch School, Herbrand Street, Holborn, arrived at the Merchant Taylors' School, where they were met by the Ashwell billeting officer, Mrs Phyllis Fordham, and the Ashwell doctors, John and Sheila Moynihan, who had hurried back from holiday to examine the children, who were aged from five to eleven, each carrying a cardboard box containing a gas mask. During the head inspection, a number of the children were found to have nits, so it was decided that these children must be isolated until the nits had been exterminated. Mrs Fordham's sister, Mrs Barbara Hill of Elbrook House, undertook this task but after a few days she called in the doctor because the nits had taken refuge in her hair.

Peter Mason, six years of age, was found to have a temperature so the nurse decided to take him, with his brother John, aged nine, to the Parish Room and, if he was quite well the next morning, it was agreed that the two boys should come to live with me and my wife, at Dixies cottage. We had only been married a few months and here we were, with two foster children and every bed in the cottage filled.

Then came children from two other London schools, to be checked and fitted into Ashwell households: the pupils of Bloomsbury Technical School, together with teachers and helpers, and children from Brompton Oratory, escorted by three nuns.

Eventually all the children were found homes: Dr Sheila Moynihan took in four teachers and her parents, Mr and Mrs Ferguson, at the Chantry House accepted the three nuns. This latter arrangement did not prove to be very successful. It is well known that as we males become senior citizens we have certain problems with our plumbing. Mr Ferguson found that whenever he needed to make a call to the one bathroom in the house, one of the nuns had beaten him to it! After all the children had settled down to their new life, their parents came down on Sundays and were catered for in the Parish Room.

Arrangements were made between Mr Geoffrey Whitby, Headmaster of the Merchant Taylors' School, Miss Anne Hyslop, Headmistress of the Junior School and the Evacuee Teachers for the education of the children. Some teaching took place in the Village Hall and The Bushel and Strike Clubroom; the latter became known as St George's Hall and was fitted out as a canteen for the evacuees, with Mrs Violet Crack in charge.

Soon came a further invasion, this time some pupils from Eastbourne Grammar School. Their education was continued at Hitchin Grammar School.

Marie Whitby, the Headmaster's daughter, contributes the following reminiscences:

"As we lived in the school, we saw a lot of the evacuees who shared the building. I remember their arrival, as we peered out of the big drawing-room window; they looked a sad bunch, assembled on the triangle of grass outside the church gate, and people kept arriving and looking them over before going off with their choice. I felt very sorry for them, particularly the last two, brother and sister, red haired; fortunately Mrs Covington, our nanny, who had not intended to offer a home, took pity on them, and I know they were very happy with her, because they still come back to Ashwell to visit, although she died years ago. (Her husband, Ralph Covington, was the road sweeper.)Some of the evacuees thought strawberries grew on trees and milk was born in bottles. The funniest incident was when one boy ran in to Father (we kept two pigs as well as sheep and rabbits, for the war effort) and said, "Sir, come quickly - there's a lot of little pigs in the stye blowing up a big pig!". A very graphic description of piglets suckling, we thought.

"Another thing I remember particularly, as a Girl Guide, is collecting a mile of pennies, which necessitated the whole Guide company guarding the contributions, laid end to end all the way up the High Street - quite a palaver. The next time we did it, Father drew numerous large circles on the ground, the circumferences adding up to a mile, more or less, which only needed one attendant! The money went to the Spitfire Fund.

"I also remember having a fete in our garden, organised by my brother (8) and me (9) at which we sold all our old toys and raffled a large marrow, and raised £2.03 for Mrs Ferguson's sea-boot stocking fund.

"At the start of the war, we were asked to collect metal, which we were told would be melted down to make Spitfires. In a fit of patriotism Father 'donated' all our saucepans, including some aluminium double-pans and steamers, which we are still regretting. A huge pile of pans grew in the playground at Merchant Taylors' School, as the whole village arrived with contributions. Father took the opportunity to remove the iron railings from the wall of the front garden, which he had long wished to do, but Mrs Fordham hadn't let him!"

Meanwhile the Observer Corps (later the Royal Observer Corps) were ever on the alert at their post on Kingsland Way which these volunteers manned 24 hours a day; in fact, from 24 August 1939 they had tracked every plane which had passed over Ashwell and estimated its height and type.

At about the same time, our neighbours at Steeple Morden had received about 100 evacuee children and Doctor Sheila had set up a clinic, known as the Felicity Mary Clinic, in Hay Street. Little did the children or even the Doctor dream of the events that were to take place in our peaceful villages.

In 1937 the powers that be had decided that a major airfield was to be built at Bassingbourn, with Steeple Morden as a satellite.

The Steeple Morden farmers were furious, when they were told that three hundred acres of their best agricultural land were to be covered with concrete. In spite of their protests, the runways were built, at a cost of about £180,000, by hundreds of British and Irish workers, using thousands of tons of Bedfordshire ballast, brought in by John Inns' lorries through Ashwell's High Street where, sadly, Lucy Cooper's little daughter was knocked down by one of them and killed.

To protect the workers from daylight attacks by enemy aircraft, the RAF had an armoured car fitted with machine guns.

The airfield was bounded on the south side by Ashwell Street (which was closed to the public). If you look on any Ordnance Survey map you will see Ashwell Street (the old spelling was Strete) stretching from the old A14 near Bassingbourn and ending at Partridge Hill, Ashwell.

A bomb store was built on the airfield and there was also storage for 72,000 gallons of high octane fuel.

Some 560 airfields were built by about 60,000 men in Great Britain. In 1939 11 RAF Operating Training Unit (OTU) moved in, with Anson and Wellington bombers. Pilot training started, even before the runways and buildings had been completed. In fact, the hangars and control tower were not built until 1943.

Most of the facts and figures covering Steeple Morden I have gleaned from Ken Wells, who kindly allowed me to read the manuscript of his excellent story, A VILLAGE AIRFIELD AT WAR*, which I recommend to you and indeed any student of wartime Britain.

The Wellington bomber, with two 145 horsepower engines and a wing span of 86 feet, weighed ten tons.

On take off, one of these planes hit a steam roller, knocking the driver off his seat. Unfortunately, there were many accidents, injuries and deaths.

Early in the war, 20 Wellingtons were lost in a few days at Bassingbourn. Some bombs were dropped by mistake on both airfields, by our own planes. One pilot thought he was over Germany, having mistaken the Thames for the Rhine, and dropped three bombs on Bassingbourn, fortunately without damage. On the other hand, one night a slightly damaged Junkers 88 landed on Steeple Morden airfield; when a vigilant Special Constable saw the swastika on its tail he ran like hell. The crew were soon taken prisoner, and after telling their captors

---

*Obtainable from the publisher, Egon Publishers Ltd, 15 Royston Road, Baldock, or any bookshop. Price £14.50 (plus postage £1.00). ISBN 0 905858 87 5.

RATION BOOK

R.B.1
16

MINISTRY OF
FOOD
1953-1954

M of F

SERIAL NO,
AD 843030

Ended may 8
1954

Surname......................... Initials.................

Address *Milton Cottage*

West End Ashwell

Nr. Baldock Herts

F.O. CODE No.

IF FOUND
RETURN TO
ANY FOOD
OFFICE

L. Haylock Ashwell

Above and below the 1953-54 Ration Book of Len Haylock, who was for many years a museum helper.
(Museum)

John and Peter Mason, our evacuees from September 1st, 1939. (Mrs. A. W. Sheldrick)

6 ENTER NAMES AND ADDRESSES OF RETAILERS

MEAT *T. D. DENNIS HIGH ST ASHWELL HERTS*

EGGS *C. H. WESTROPE HIGH ST. ASHWEAL HERTS*

FATS *C. H. WESTROPE HIGH ST. ASHWELL HERTS*

CHEESE *C. H. WESTROPE HIGH ST ASHWELL HEATS*

BACON *C. H. WESTROPE HIGH ST ASHWELL HERTS*

SUGAR *C. H. WESTROPE HIGH STREET ASHWELL*

SPARE

If Coupons Deposited Retailer Enters "D"   If Coupons Deposited Retailer Enters "D"

*Fill in if you deposit sections with retailer

R.B.1
16

TEA

If you deposit this page fill in overleaf

	52	50
	TEA 13 13 TEA	TEA 13 13 TEA

	12	11	10	9	8	7	6	5	4	3	2	1
EGGS			3				2					1

*Surname and Initials

	12	11	10	9	8	7	6	5	4	3	2	1
FATS B M CF			3				2					1

*Surname and Initials

	12	11	10	9	8	7	6	5	4	3	2	1
CHEESE			3				2					1

*Surname and Initials

	12	11	10	9	8	7	6	5	4	3	2	1
BACON			3				2					1

*Surname and Initials

	12	11	10	9	8	7	6	5	4	3	2	1
SUGAR		S R	Q 3			S R	Q 2			S R	Q 1	

*Surname and Initials

that Britain could not win the war, they refused to eat for a few days, which meant extra rations for the RAF! In addition to the first aid lectures to the Ashwell Home Guard, Air Raid Wardens and other bodies, the Doctors John and Sheila were also involved with the same services at Steeple Morden.

The first big raid on the London docks was on Saturday, 7 September, 1940. While the Steeple Morden Home Guards watched the awesome golden red glow in the sky from their look out post on top of Saundersons Mill, Ashwellians watched from Claybush trees.

By the middle of September 1939 petrol was rationed and National Registration Identity cards, which had to be carried at all times, were issued to everyone. Sandbags to smother incendiary bombs were delivered to every house.

"You will be home before the leaves have fallen from the trees", Kaiser Wilhelm had told the German troops in 1914 as they left for the front line. Here in Britain in 1939 the know-alls said, "It won't last long, six months at the most", and there were those who had visited Germany. "We will soon beat them, their tanks are only made of three-ply." Little did they know that we had three-ply planes and dummy anti- aircraft guns made from sheet metal and wood to try to deceive the enemy. Then to add to our problems, snow fell early in December and we had frost almost nightly from Christmas until February 1940, and in January a blizzard blocked all the roads in and out of Ashwell for a week.

London tea merchants, Ferguson and Hollness, evacuated their London office staff to Jessamine House, with Mr Tonge and Mr Patten in charge. Mr Tonge was instructed by Lord Woolton, the Minister of Food, to find storage buildings in this area for large quantities of tea.

Tea was not the only food stored on a large scale in Ashwell: tons of lard was kept in the old Bear Farm buildings, giving the Parish Council much cause for concern, especially with the loss of some of its firefighting equipment.

Brays, the builders, were asked to repair and waterproof the Jessamine House barn which was soon filled with chests of tea ten feet high. The aircraft hangar at Odsey [which was built for Leslie Leroy Irvin, the parachute pioneer and founder of the famous parachute firm at Letchworth], the barns at Ringstead and many others in the area became tea warehouses. The firm's special blend, 'Dongalla Tips Tea', was later stocked by Westrope's, the Ashwell Grocers and Provisions Merchants.

Sir Arnold Wilson, the Conservative Member of Parliament for the Hitchin constituency, had joined the Royal Air Force in October, 1939. Sir Arnold had been criticised for his friendship with Nazi leaders

and although I rather think he was above the normal age for flying duties, he became the rear gunner in a Wellington bomber.

Next came a set of government instructions: "All sections of WVS Civil Defence and Air Raid Precautions must be ready to provide accommodation for people rendered homeless, caused by unexploded bombs or gas contamination etc"; and advice to wearers of spectacles: "Obtain spectacles over which the gas mask can be fitted". Spectacle wearers in the forces were issued with a suitable type of metal frame, and had regular gas mask drill.

In 1940, food rationing was introduced. The weekly ration per person was 4 oz bacon, 2 oz butter, 2 oz tea, meat worth 1s 2d (2 small chops or 3/4 lb stewing beef), 1 egg per fortnight. Cheese, sugar and fats were also rationed. Margarine was 8d to 10d per pound. Eggs, when you could find them, 10 for 6d. Bread was not rationed, dried egg-powder could be bought, but coffee was unobtainable.

The year 1940 was a terrible time for Britain, although worse for others. The Nazis invaded Denmark and Norway; the Netherlands and Belgium fell; Italy, our ally in the First World War declared war on Britain and France, the latter partitioned into occupied France and Vichy France, governed by Marshal Petain.

The Lord Mayor of London set up an Air Raid Distress Fund. All towns and villages were asked to subscribe to it. John Newsom, the County Education Officer, visited schools throughout the county to advise on air-raid precautions for children, as some parents threatened to take their children away from school unless shelters were provided. John Bailey of Westbury House dug out an entrance on his lawn to the old Page's Brewery cellars for the use of West End folks as an air-raid shelter.

In May, due to the sinking of so many cargo ships, there was a paper shortage; householders were asked to save all clean newspapers, to be collected by the dustmen and in June our Member of Parliament, Sir Arnold Wilson's plane was shot down and he was reported missing. The Local Defence Volunteers (LDV) was formed and a system of fire watching against enemy attacks was ordered.

In July, the Ministry of Food, anxious to ensure that surplus fruit from gardens and allotments was not wasted, instructed that local arrangements be made to collect either in the raw state or in the form of jam and bottled fruit by Women's Institutes or other local bodies. Permits were given for extra sugar for the purpose, and bee-keepers were allowed sugar to feed their bees in winter.

In September, funds were raised to build more of the famous Spitfire fighter planes. There were collections of cash and any kind of aluminium; saucepans, milk bottle tops, etc. Letchworth raised £5,000. An exhibition of fragments of bombs, an unexploded incendiary bomb and other bits and pieces connected with the war was held at Bennett's works in Letchworth. There was a searchlight unit near Beverly Farm, which may have caused a Hurricane fighter to crash, just behind Steeple Morden church; fortunately the pilot escaped and young Aubrey Wright gave him a lift on his bike to the nearest telephone. Then Aubrey dashed back to the blazing plane to warn the onlookers of the danger of exploding ammunition.

Then there was what the locals called the 'Wednesday bomber' which came over regularly on Wednesdays, but this time flew low over the village and dropped a land mine in a field off Trap Lane, Steeple Morden, causing a crater big enough to have accommodated the nearby Green Man Pub. How fortunate that it dropped so far from the village. Other Ashwellians nicknamed it 'Old Faithful', as it would circle round the Church Tower to get its bearings for a bombing run on the neighbouring airfields. It may have been the same plane about which Dr Sheila Moynihan writes as follows: "During the war I was a civilian Medical Officer and always on call to the two aerodromes. I was given a special pass to go between Steeple Morden and Bassingbourn as the intervening road was closed at night.

I also recall that just after midnight on 22 July 1941 a Junkers 88 was rammed by a Canadian pilot who was under training at Steeple Morden. Most of the Wellington came down in a field of ripe barley next to our garden and burst into flames, the heat of the burning plane making it impossible for me to do anything. The Junkers fell in a field on the other side of Ashwell Street and a clip of machine gun bullets fell on our doorstep. We were under guard for three days when no one was allowed to approach until all the bodies had been found." Arthur Kirchin, a member of the Royal Observer Corps, said the JU88 was based in Holland and as the pilot was believed to have been a Cambridge undergraduate, he had a very good knowledge of this area and was believed to have been responsible for a number of successful sorties over East Anglia.

Stanley Revill told me quite recently that on the morning of 22 July he, a teenager at the time, went with a friend to see the wreckage. In Hunts Close, the field behind the Lucas Lane bungalows, he saw the bodies of two German airmen. Stanley remembers especially the hands of the pilot which he said were smooth and perfectly manicured, and that he was decorated with the Iron Cross. At 7.30 the next morning I was sent to repair some damaged roofs. I saw the propeller of one of the planes propped up against what used to be the Wagon and Horses Pub at Springhead. There were several holes through the slated roof of Playground Cottage adjoining the Recreation Ground.

PC Legge, Ashwell's resident Police Officer, told me that he caught a man taking home the Wellington's radio set.

When Roy York, well known as a writer for Radio and Television, heard about the forthcoming publication of this book, he sent us the following reminiscence entitled 'Anecdotes of an Evacuee'.

I was one of the many lucky children to be evacuated to Ashwell in 1939. After an initial billet which only lasted a few weeks, I was eventually placed with Bill and Phoebe Barton.

The country was a world most London children knew very little or nothing about. We were suddenly surrounded by fruit, eggs, water, fields, haystacks, cow-plops and mud.

Some of us went mad. Our eagerness to eat as many apples as possible, jump up and down on haystacks, tear our clothes, get covered in dirt, fight and make a lot of noise was bound to have upset some villagers. Our behaviour must have been particularly trying to those kind people who had taken us into their homes. One slight restraint in my case was that I lived opposite Mr Legge, the village policeman.

My ultimate folly was the morning after a Junkers 88 collided in mid-air with a Wellington bomber. Parts of both crews and wreckage of the aircraft were spread over a wide area, much of it on land behind the Cricketers Inn and in the fields next to the Appleton house.

Eddie Trusson, another evacuee, and I decided we must get some souvenirs. Two days later Mr Legge called. With Bill and Phoebe Barton present we all stood in the little living-room of Number 4, Station Road.

'What have you got from the wreckage?' he asked.

Mr Legge stared straight at me.

I tried to avoid his eyes. 'Nothing.' 'Don't lie to me', he said loudly. 'Ronnie (he named a village boy) said you showed him a belt of machine-gun bullets.' I felt my face flush at being caught out.

'Come on, Roy. What have you got?' Phoebe asked quietly.

I told them.

As Mr Legge removed the last of the three boxes of live bullets and cannon shells from our shed, I heard him say, 'That wee devil has enough ammunition here to blow up the street!' After the policeman had gone, Bill Barton told me off firmly. He never raised his voice or his hand. The Barton's patience was almost unlimited. I was a very lucky evacuee.

I also remember village girls. What devastation some of these young beauties brought to our eleven year old hearts.

There was one in particular. I always endeavoured to be standing next to the recreation ground as she returned home from school in the hope of attracting her attention. Several weeks went by and my patience was eventually rewarded by a smile. Then joy upon joy, after a few more days, she spoke.

Some weeks later she was one of our group as we splashed and played in the cold, clear water of the Springs. Billy Nicholson, another evacuee, was also there. At the time he was my best mate. The only reservation I had about him was the sneaking suspicion that he also had a fancy for the girl I'd set my heart on.

Billy moved along the bank of the river and climbed a tree. As he edged himself along a branch, he shouted, 'Look at this!' He gripped the tree limb with both hands and swung himself backwards and forwards high above the water.

I looked at the object of my desire and saw she was impressed. Not to be outdone, I waited until Billy got down then went to the same tree. I selected a branch and called, 'I can do that!' Why I didn't think to use the same branch I'll never know.

As I clasped a bough and hung with both hands, I was horrified to feel it bend. Slowly and inevitably it sagged lower and lower. At first it was only my feet that got wet but the branch continued its descent until the water was up to my chest. Eventually I let go, crawled up the bank past the laughing children and made my dripping way up the steps to the street.

Humiliation made me avoid her for quite a while after that and by the time we spoke again my ardour had completely cooled."

The war intensifies

The government hastily drew up plans for an expected invasion. All towns and village name signs were taken down and the 'Ashwell' on the Village Hall, Parish Council and Museum Notice Boards was painted out. The conspicuous yellow and black circular signs, bearing the name Ashwell on the Newnham and Station roads, put up by the Automobile Association, were taken down, never to return, together with all fingerposts pointing to towns or villages.

Heavy bombing was expected, followed by the landing of paratroops. Martial law would be proclaimed immediately.

Householders would be instructed that water must be saved, toilets would not be flushed and latrines would be dug in gardens. Civilians would not be allowed on any main road, to allow the free passage of military traffic.

Ashwell men and women travelled by bus or bicycle to Baldock, where the Kayser Bondor factory (now Tesco's Supermarket) and Quenby's Garage were making or assembling small fittings for the war effort, and Frank Newman and Sons were making bomb casings, which were tested on Salisbury Plain. At Letchworth, Kryn and Lahey were producing bomb and shell cases. The Spirella corset factory's machines were working full time, stitching parachute fabric for the Irvin Parachute Company, who assembled and supplied the complete article to the RAF. Dixons were turning out precision parts, and bearings by Chater Lea. Lewis Falk's machines made embroidered insignia and flashes for service uniforms.

1940 will be remembered for the evacuation of 300,000 British and Allied

Bob Davis Herts and Beds & RMP
(Museum)

Jack Geeves RASC (Museum)

Charles Revill RAP (Museum)

Alan Picking (RA) 1944. Served
in North Africa. (Alan Picking)

Mary Clements   *Christopher Clements*

Mary Clements (ATS) and twin brother
Christopher (RN) (Rev. Pickard who
later married Mary)

Some Ashwellians who
served in the
Second World War

Lawrence Bryant (RAF) served
in Middle East. (Museum)

L-r: Three National Servicemen Terry Crump (Army), Gordon Gentle (Navy) and
David Seaby (RAF) (Marjorie Gentle)

Captain W. H. Fordham and Sergeant W. Andrews lead the march along the High Street of the Home Guard, Civil Defence and Red Cross personnel, a number of whom were veterans of World War I. (1942) (Marjorie Gentle)

Ashwell Home Guard, on the Recreation Ground. 1940's L to R: W. Huffer, Sen. A. Covington, S. Sheldrick, S. Edwards, F. Livings, B. Seaby, V. Worboys, H. Moule, W. Livings, Sen. H. Sheldrick, E. Hankin, A. Huffer, W. Livings, B. Game. B. Hankin, Jun. B. Worboys, E. Ashby. Unknown, Unknown. Middle row: Sun Collins, S. Brown, Unknown, L. James, A. Gallant, W. Glassock, W. James, S. Worboys, W. Law, E. Wilkins, Uknown, R. Fordham, W. Picking, J. Ashby, M. White. R. Christy. Front row: B. Hankin, Sen. A. Furr, S. Revel, H. Skerman, Unknown, A. Harradine, G. Turner, Unknown, G. Revels, Sen, W. Barton, B. Harvey, S. Waldock, A. Hall, C. Levings, G. Berry, J. Geeves, K. Bryant, R. Davis. (G. Berry)

troops from Dunkirk by the heroic skippers of the hundreds of pleasure boats, yachts and little ships which faced shell fire from the shores and bombs from the air between 26 May and 3 June, which Winston Churchill described as "This miracle of deliverance". Tom Smith of Newnham told me that he, with hundreds more, scrambled aboard a paddle-steamer and was pushed further on until his back was against the funnel, when a bomb was dropped down the funnel, splitting his ear drums.

Things did not improve in 1941. Hitler invaded Russia but, like Napoleon, was eventually driven back. Bombs were constantly dropped on Malta and Hitler's deputy, Rudolph Hess, flew into Britain to arrange peace terms! In February, War Weapons Week took place and the government decided to conscript women. The Local Defence Volunteers were renamed the Home Guard and in June held a recruiting drive. In some areas, due to the shortage of rifles, pikes or pickaxe shafts and even dummy rifles made of wood were issued.

As most of the members of Toc H were in the forces, their meeting place, the old Page's Brewery stables, was handed over to the Scouts, who shared it with the Home Guard. The latter used it for training and lectures. Doctor Sheila Moynihan told me that she was invited to give some lectures on first aid. On one occasion, while she was explaining how to treat a patient suffering a haemorrhage, three men fainted and were dragged outside to recover in the fresh air! One exercise, undertaken by the Home Guard, was to convey 'casualties' to Ringstead (at that time the home of Mrs Cones) which was to act as a hospital. To make it as real as possible, the doctor was sent for, to attend the 'casualties'. Dr Sheila told me that, as she drove through the gates at Ringstead, a strange camouflaged figure jumped out in front of her. It was the Home Guard Commander, Captain W H Fordham.

Toolmaker, George Berry, who had come to Ashwell in 1938 and married Dorothy Gray (daughter of Mr Edward Gray, Mrs Wolverley Fordham's chauffeur and general factotum for 56 years) played a key rôle in the Home Guard, being in charge of its mobile section - mainly young men in reserved occupations. Sunday mornings were spent Drilling and Manoeuvring. When the church clock struck 12 noon, it was straight into the Bushel and Strike.

When they were first formed, these hardy volunteers were issued with Lee Enfield rifles but no ammunition. However, a piece of string and five crackers made enough noise to frighten the birds. Perhaps, as George says, many thought any invading Germans would die of laughing! On one occasion, when a mock invasion of Ashwell by Hinxworth's Dad's Army had been planned, Stan Brown was detailed to hide in a ditch on their expected route and signal back to the Headquarters at the Brewery when he saw them. The Hinxworth contingent suddenly appeared without warning in Gardiners Lane and attacked the Brewery. Later, a post-mortem was held in the Bushel and Strike and Stan Brown boasted of his sharpness in spotting the approach of the invaders, watching them pass him, so pleased he had not been spotted. The only thing was - he'd forgotten to send a warning signal.

A somewhat crude anti tank weapon - known as the Northover Projector - was issued to the Home Guard. It consisted of a long tube, 3" in diameter, mounted on a tripod with a breach block. The other end of the tube was fitted with a ring sight. The general idea was to fire a bottle filled with an inflammable liquid with a charge behind it to send it on its way - maximum range 200 yards. On impact the bottle would explode and the enemy tank engulfed in flames. At its first demonstration, 'Skip' Picking, whose favourite expression was "bugger it", was detailed to fire it with Cliff Levings the loader. Skip pulled the trigger, the bottle shot up the tube. Unfortunately, the screw attaching the sight ring projected inside the tube, shattering the bottle which exploded in flames. 'Skip', in a panic, opened the breach, resulting in the ball of fire shooting into his lap. The air was blue with his favourite expression.

Pauline Whitby remembers:

"During - I think - the second year of the war there was a lot of anxiety about possible infiltration by parachutists or a Fifth Column, and the Home Guard planned a practice exercise in detecting them. Various people were to impersonate the enemy; they had either to come from outside the village or to be in disguise. At my father's suggestion I wore a pair of trousers borrowed from Mr Knowles, who ran the Bushel and Strike, and who was about my height, and my brother's school cap, and hid my 'bomb' inside my gas-mask case. This was a tin one; the bottom was loose because it was always getting dropped.

"The 'bombs' were small sand-bags, small enough to hide in one's hand. The objectives to be reached included the Telephone Exchange and Home Guard HQ which was in the Brewery offices. I didn't even know where the Telephone Exchange was, but my Father explained that it was the small building on the alley between the Museum and the Technical Room (Alms Lane). A Home Guard was to be posted at each end of the alley. Father masterminded my attack. The Technical Room also referred to elsewhere as the Parish Rooms or Church Room was being used as a cafeteria for the parents of the evacuees; he suggested that I should walk straight through it and out of the back door. I did this without difficulty, hurled my sand-bag, and went out again and round to the alley. I was stopped by the Home Guard but explained that I was going to reclaim my bomb. This was in the rules, so he had to give it back to me.

"Shortly afterwards I was stopped and the 'bomb' confiscated. I went and collected a spare, put it inside my gas-mask, and made for the Brewery. Here I was stopped again and searched. I proffered the gas-mask case upside down and the searcher removed the bottom lid, exposing the canister of the gas-mask, but did not think to turn it the other way up. Being obviously in disguise I was marched in to Captain Fordham, who was sitting at a table by the wall of the offices. I dropped the case, the lid fell off and the sand-bag slid out. I picked it up and hurled it at the wall.

"Captain Fordham pointed out that I would have been killed by the blast and damaged nothing but the wall. I believe the official report said that Home Guard HQ had been successfully defended, but I still think I had scored."

The Air Raid Wardens from their headquarters at the Parish Room were kept busy patrolling the streets at night, to check that all windows were completely blacked out. Everyone was expected to stick strips of gummed brown paper on their windows to minimise the danger of flying glass. All street lighting was cut off, the windows of railway carriages were blacked out, car headlamps also except for a small section, and cars were immobilised at night.

Five hundred German bombers bombed London on 16 April, 1941 and in another raid on 10 May thousands of incendiaries and high explosive bombs were dropped indiscriminately, killing 1400. St Paul's Cathedral was hit, the Chamber of the House of Commons destroyed and Big Ben hit. The square tower of Westminster Abbey fell and Westminster Hall was set on fire; and 1941 was the worst year ever for road accidents in Britain. Due to war-time restrictions on vehicle headlights, an average of 26 people died every day, 9,444 in all.

Builders were working seven days a week on defence work. Brays built several machine gun posts with brick and concrete reinforced with steel.

While we were building one at Odsey, in a copse off the Royston road, a party of army officers drove up the hill to see what was going on. One of the officers said, "The person who ordered this to be built should be shot; if I was an enemy tank commander coming along the Baldock road, this is one position I would wipe off the face of the earth, it's so obvious".

One morning we arrived to find a long white arrow pointing north, the turf had been lifted to expose the chalk below. The authorities decided the arrow on this hilltop was a pointer to Bassingbourn aerodrome for enemy aircraft and was the work of a spy or fifth columnist. We built other defence works at Wimpole, where RAF planes were hidden under the trees in the park. As Brays were then only a small firm (John Bray and several of the employees were serving in the Forces), we had to amalgamate with Rabans, the Baldock builders.

We were then switched to what was known as the second line of defence. This was a chain of reinforced block houses or pillboxes which were built to house anti-tank guns with additional rifle and machine gun slits. We did a section in the Debden and Audley End area, working from 7.00 am to 7.00 pm seven days a week. The Royal Engineers sent a team to camouflage each blockhouse, one as a cowshed with a thatched roof; I remember this blockhouse very well. After the concrete had set very hard a party of soldiers brought an anti-tank gun to fit in the opening, which had been carefully made according to the drawings supplied. The gun would not fit in. After several site meetings with very bad language from our side, we were told to enlarge the hole to the size given on a new drawing. I had the job, with hammer and chisel and hacksaw (for the steel rods) and bloody knuckles. Even if we had an electric drill, which was almost unheard of in those days, there was no power within a mile. Later on, when I was in the army, I discovered this was known as 'organised chaos'; but this was followed by an even bigger 'cock-up'. The site foreman argued with the authority that one blockhouse which was to be built right on the river bank was shown in the drawing facing inland instead of towards the enemy. 'Build as shown', he was told, and we did, to the great amusement of two high-ranking officers who came to inspect the finished article. "We will just have to tell Mr Hitler to come round the back", was one of the senior officers' comments. A further drawing was then prepared showing a 'curtain wall' to be built, allowing the defenders to enter the blockhouse safely. I am well aware that this official 'organised chaos' does not compare with some of the post-war stuff. You may remember when Bedfordshire County Council had to demolish their half-built County Hall because the base had not been designed to support the upper floors.

At home, posters warned, 'Careless talk costs lives', and we were all (civilians and servicemen) asked not to talk to strangers about anything to do with the war effort: the stranger could be a spy. There was the call, 'Dig for victory'. Farmers were told to plough up grassland and grow as much foodstuffs as possible - not all responded. All the Ashwell allotments were producing record crops. At The Bury, Mrs Fordham had her rose bushes dug up and filled the rose garden with fruit bushes; and her kitchen garden (where Wolverley House has since been built) was in full cultivation. As there was a great shortage of iron and steel (ships were being sunk), an order was made that all iron gates and fences be removed, for the war effort. A team of men came round to cut down the iron fences at the Congregational and Wesleyan chapels, iron fences around monuments in the churchyard, even the galvanised tubes between the elm trees at the recreation ground were taken and the iron gates from private houses. One lady a couple of miles from Ashwell craftily hid her ornamental gates and brought them out again after the war. There was fuel rationing, and to buy new clothes the outfitter snipped out the necessary number of coupons from your clothes ration book. The ringing of church bells was banned, but they were to be rung to warn the public at the first sign of an attempted invasion.

At about 4 o'clock one morning the pilot of an enemy plane, believed to be returning to base, dropped three bombs on Ashwell. Marie Whitby of Seven Springs Gallery says, "I remember waking in the night when Ashwell's three bombs fell, all within a few hundred yards of our house, and viewing the subsequent craters".

One of these bombs dropped in the Bury meadow near Redlands Grange. This was only discovered many years later when a circular hole appeared. The bomb was dug out by a bomb disposal unit. The second fell behind the thatched wall in Gardiners Lane. The third fell in Alms Lane, near the Ladies' Hairdressing Salon. The air raid wardens asleep in the Parish Room, awakened by the nearby explosion, dashed up Alms Lane and in the darkness fell into the small crater. It was rather near the electricity transformer, but fortunately only smashed the sewer pipes in the lane.

The National Fire Service came into being in 1942 and remained a National Force until 1948. Fire crews from this area were often called to help with major fires in London and other cities. De Havillands, of Hatfield, brought the Mosquito bomber into service. I believe they were built many of Balsa wood and the wings were filled with ping pong balls for lightness.

Mr Leslie Brown, who was surveyor to Baldock Urban District Council and now lives at Oversprings in Ashwell, was put in charge of several local Fire Service Units, including Ashwell.

A new pump was delivered to Ashwell and a special runway made down to The Springs; at the same time the Ashwell Parish Fire handcart with its old canvas hose was taken away, never to return.

Leo Pickett remembers when Ashwell boasted a Fire Station which was in fact a Nissen hut, sited in an orchard behind Plait Hall, at the junction of Hodwell and Church Lane.

"At this time I was a part-time member of the Auxiliary Fire Service (AFS). We met every Sunday morning for training. Butcher, Eddie Brown, was in charge of the detachment, and we took it in turns to man the fire station every night. We had a Coventry Climax trailer pump and a car to tow it. The car was so decrepit that one evening, when we were going to Luton, we all had to push it up Offley Hill. One winter's night 1942/43, with windows shut and blackouts up and the coke stove turned down low, we retired fully dressed to the bunk beds. The call of nature for one fireman roused him sufficiently to realise that the hut was full of fumes. He dragged us all out into the fresh air, preventing a terrible tragedy.

The coke stove was never turned down again.

     We were never required to attend a fire, but on a few occasions we acted as back-up for Baldock and Letchworth, when they were called out during the London blitz. After the war, the Nissen hut was used by Bob Crump as a Fish and Chip Shop".

The government issued a handbook dealing with air raid precautions and, with the fear of the enemy using poison gas, there were instructions for personal protection against gas.

Call-up

In January 1942 I was instructed to appear at St Albans for a medical; at the end I was interviewed by an ancient warrior, a grey-haired major with an impressive display of medal ribbons, who asked me which branch of the services I would prefer. As I was in the building trade, I suggested the army, Royal Engineers. "A very wise choice, that's what it shall be", the major replied. In February I received a postcard ordering me to go to Letchworth labour exchange, where I was told that I must report for work at Dunhams' Lane, Letchworth, where hostel accommodation was being built at the Government Training Centre for the naval personnel who were to be taught the intricacies of A.S.D.I.C., the anti-submarine device. I cycled to Letchworth, then worked from 7.30 am to 7.00 pm six days a week until 7 May, when I received a 'Welcome to His Majesty's army' with a very good photograph of a smiling King George VI, wearing a general's uniform which carried at least a dozen medal ribbons. The leaflet ended, 'I welcome you to the Army, Fear God, Honour the King and May Victory Soon Crown Our Arms'! I also received a railway warrant to take me to Wokingham, near Reading. After training at Arborfield, I became a gunner in a Mixed Heavy Anti Aircraft battery, and not a sapper in the Royal Engineers. Then after firing practice off the Norfolk coast, our battery was sent to gun sites in the Midlands to protect aircraft and armament factories. There were four guns on each site, either 4.5 ins guns which sent 84 lbs of high explosive to a height of eight miles in 50 seconds; or the 3.7 ins with a faster rate of fire and shells weighing 49 lbs. Two ATS were responsible for working the height and range-finder; this information was passed to the five ATS on the predictor (an early type of computer) who then passed on to the gunners the exact position the enemy plane would be when the shell reached it. ATS also manned the telephones, the crude Radar sets of those days, and the cookhouse.

    Our first gunsite was over a disused coal mine high above the black country, at a village called Oakham. With binoculars you could see Wolverhampton, West Bromwich, Smethwick and sprawling Birmingham, where the factories were all turning out the implements of war and at the same time releasing so much chemical pollution that every night our brass shell cases turned green! On the first day's tea parade, cockney Charley Brown, the medical orderly, told us to stand by our beds at 1800 hours wearing just our underpants for the Medical Officer's inspection.

    There we stood, a motley bunch of about 30 of us, coal miners, bricklayers, a bus driver, a journalist, a hairdresser, a butler and a city gent, aged between 18 and 33, the long, the short and the tall. The lady MO, about 22 years of age, with a quick order of "Drop your pants" proceed to inspect each man, using a pencil to lift up certain parts.

There were long periods of boredom and then a few nights of action. Ready to man the guns 24 hours a day and short of men, we were only allowed out of camp one day in eleven from 10.00 hours to 1700 hours.

An inspection by the Princess Royal caused quite a stir; we worked all through one dark night. Whitewash was splashed around the kerbs and the edges of the fuel dump, the hut stoves were painted black and the ATS worked all night sewing new bow and arrow flashes on the battle dress blouses. Some were given notepaper and envelopes and sent to the rest room to write home to mother during the visit. I was sent to paint the RA gun at the foot of the flag staff with one of the guards holding a torch. Then at daybreak I was told to make holes in the grass for an officer to drop in daffodils freshly bought from a Dudley florist. Her Royal Highness said she was impressed but I feel sure she was bored with it all. The day ended with the best army meal I ever had.

On Sunday, 28 June, 1942 Wellington R1445 took off from Steeple Morden at 17.45 hours and circled over Ashwell, when suddenly there was trouble with one engine and at 1750 hours it crashed, destroying one pair of Council houses on Station Road, the home of Mrs Revill adjoining that of Mr and Mrs S Bryant. Mrs Revill's son, Stanley, remembers it well and said that it was fortunate that both his mother and the Bryants were out at the time. Pilot Officer J E Casey from New Zealand and his mechanic, LAC R L Wilson, were both killed.

The Herts & Beds Pictorial reported on 30.0.42: "Cottages Razed" Mr and Mrs Sidney Bryant and Mrs Revills were absent from their homes at Station Road, Ashwell on Sunday morning. They received a message to return, and on arrival found that their homes had been completely destroyed by fire. The brigades from Letchworth and Baldock, and Civil Defence personnel of Ashwell cleared the debris".

Note: Due to wartime censorship, the press were not allowed to give the true facts.

The very next day, 29 June, Wellington X3173 crashed on the field, just beyond Reg Fitzgerald's garage, known as Paddocks.

One of the oldest and most battered of the Wellington trainers at Steeple Morden crashed on the airfield, and as the fire crew set off to douse the flames, there were cries from the ground staff, "Let the poor old sod die".

One event which gave us a glimmer of hope was the defeat of Rommel's forces at El Alamein in 1942.

The Americans arrive

On Sunday, 25 October, 1942 the fiftieth anniversary of this turning point in the war, the Duke of Kent and Prime Minister, John Major, attended a service together with a large number of Allied and German war Veterans at Alamein cemetery to remember, as Robert Fisk wrote on 26 October 1992 in the Independent, '12,000 Allied names without bodies and the estimated 11,000 German and Italian bodies up the coast road'. Then after reading this inscription on one grave stone, 'Some day we'll understand', he turned to ask 79 year old WO 1st class Andrew Ellis, 'What would they understand'? Andrew, wearing his poppy-red Chelsea Pensioner's coat, replied, 'There has been war for 2,000 years and there will always be wars until people stop fighting for economic and political reasons'.

The second big event of 1942 was the arrival of the United States Army Air Force. In October the Americans brought their huge B17F bombers to RAF Bassingbourn and between 7 November 1942 and 25 April 1945 these Flying Fortresses flew 340 missions over enemy territory. The air crews were supported by a huge ground staff of mechanics, fitters, doctors, nurses, orderlies and cooks with canteens and shops, far superior to the British NAAFI (Navy Army and Air Force Institute).

Irvins, the Letchworth parachute makers, took over one room at the Three Tuns, where a number of local women, including my wife, were employed making parts for parachutes.

During 1943 Britain held a special week called Wings for Victory. Germany was attacked from the air day and night by a huge force of Allied bombers, whilst at home the Minister of Food ordered that the staff of life, the daily bread, should contain only 12% white flour and would be known as the National loaf.

In 1943 Steeple Morden became a front line aerodrome for the American 355th Fighter Group; P47 Thunderbolts and P51 Mustang fighters escorted the bombers on raids over Germany and in the last year of the war planes from Steeple Morden played an important part in what was known as ground strafing as British and American forces gradually pushed the enemy back.

To remember and honour the many United States airmen who came to live, and fly and die from these Cambridgeshire villages, a Memorial stands on the roadside between Steeple Morden and Litlington, built and cared for by the members of the East Anglian Aviation Society and to which regularly come, but in ever decreasing numbers, parties of grey-haired men who flew from here fifty years ago.

John Bray, who had been stationed in the north of England with a searchlight unit since early in the war, was suddenly released by the army, as were quite a number, and ordered to report to a secret site in Kent, taking with him a hammer and saw. There he was employed with a whole army of carpenters, scaffolders and other building workers on a hush-hush project.

Later on in the war they discovered that they had built sections of the Mulberry Harbours which were floated across the channel to be used for the landing of men and supplies during the invasion.

It was during the war that school dinners began. With the men in the forces and their wives on war work, it was found necessary to provide children with a mid day meal, a main course and sweet, which often consisted of stew, potatoes and cabbage, followed by a milk pudding. The meal cost 4d per day, 2/- per week. St George's Hall (The Bushel and Strike) and the Village Hall were both used as school canteens. For civilians, the Ministry of Food set up restaurants called National restaurants in most towns, where a simple meal could be bought at a reasonable price.

The governments of Poland, Czechoslovakia, Holland, Belgium, France and Norway were in exile in London, each with their own armed forces.

Above: *Pearl Glasscock (now Williams) accompanies a U.S.A.F. Violinist on the family harmonium. Note the blacked out window and war progress map.* (Pearl Williams)

Right: *A 1944 photo of Kathleen Westrope taken by a U.S. soldier "off the cuff". When he returned to Ashwell with the picture developed, he called in at Westrope's to find out who she was, and was surprised that it was the boss's daughter!* (Louie Harradine)

Ashwell Boy Cadets 1942-43. Back row L to R: Albert Stanton, Vince Hemmings, Reg Levitt, ? Smith, Peter Whitby, Ron Bowen, Ray Skerman, Terry Crump, Vicky Ward. Middle, second row boys: Ronnie Bird, Tony Bullock, Bob Street, Bob Bird, Robin Beadle, Jim Smith, Phil Crump, Dick Rigby, George Worboys.
Ashwell Girl Cadets, 1942-43. Back row L to R: *Dot Turner, Betty Huffer, Mrs Whitby, Mr Whitby, Miss Crainford, ? Newbury, Phylis Robbins, Eileen Brown. Front row: Sheila Rigby, Dot Furr, Pearl Glasscock, Molly Smith, Pauline Whitby, Nora Tomlin, Doreen Pearce.*
(Pearl Williams)

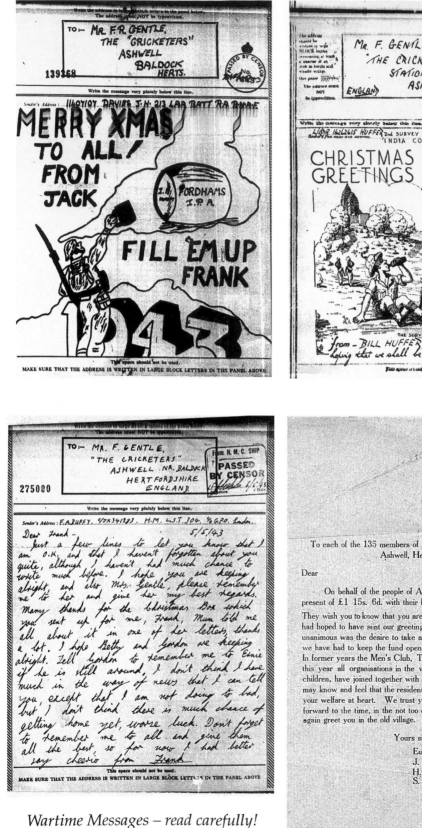

Wartime Messages – read carefully!
(Marjorie Gentle)

In February 1944 General Eisenhower set up the Supreme Headquarters Allied Expeditionary Force, and plans were prepared for the invasion of Europe, some good and some not so good.

Commando raids were made on the French coast.

Then came the massive preparations for the greatest invasion ever: the build up of tanks, guns, lorries and men. The roadsides and woods from Ipswich down to Felixstowe were packed. Forces' canteens in the area were swamped with hungry and thirsty men.

At the Ipswich station canteen, tea was served in jam jars. From the Trimley gun site we watched each morning as the landing craft swept silently down the river Orwell and disappeared out to sea and we wondered, each morning, could this be the great day. But each day they came back until 5 June when we were informed, 'All leave is cancelled', and we knew. There was very little sleep that night. Just after midnight the alarm bells rang and the barrels of our four guns (now operated by remote control) followed a fleet of heavily- loaded bombers out to sea. The USA pilots often flashed the colours, just in case we mistook them for enemy planes. Then from the Ipswich road we heard the roar of tank and lorry engines as they wound their way down to Felixstowe, where part of that great fleet of 4,000 landing craft and 700 ships was waiting to transport them over to Normandy to attack the enemy forces and eventually liberate the peoples of Europe.

Britain remembered with 'Salute the Soldier' Week; the wags called it 'Shoot the Soldier' Week. Then we had a searchlight brought on to the site to focus on enemy planes. Unfortunately, an enemy fighter flew down the beam and shot out the light, but miraculously the crew were not killed.

There was the night when our four guns had each sent up four rounds when the cry came over the tannoy, 'Cease loading, Mosquito, Cease loading'. The Mosquito had flashed the wrong colours for that period! On 13 June, 1944 the first of Hitler's secret weapons, the FZG 76, soon known to us as the 'Diver' and to civilians as the 'Doodle bug', fell at Gravesend; then, after a break of two days, 244 were launched but only 144 flew over the coast of Britain, and only 73 reached London. Our AA guns shot down 25, and fighter planes 7. About 1300 3.7 ins guns and Bofors light AA guns were used against the diver. By mid-July, 1,192 V.1s had been shot down but some still got through. Then, no doubt pressed by Prime Minister Churchill, General Sir Frederick Pile, GOC-in-Chief AA Command, decided to line the east coast with AA guns, with fighter planes behind them. This mass movement of guns, ammunition and equipment, together with 23,000 gunners and ATS took only three days. The guns were manned night and day. One problem was that the V1 could fly below the radar's search line until a new, less complicated set was brought in, and a new type of fuse. We spent a whole night removing the fuses from our shells and replacing them with a new sensitive type which could destroy an object from quite a distance, with the result that by the end of August the guns shot down 83% of the doodle bugs. On 31 August our guns shot down 90 out of the 97 destroyed that day.

The engine of one of the bugs cut out over our site and it dropped in a field, the explosion cut off an acre of beans to ground level. Another one, when hit, cut out right overhead, but as we dashed for cover the engine started up again and according to the timing, I was told, later fell near Henlow. Most days our site commander dashed off to an inquest at Felixstowe. The inquest was attended also by a naval officer and an RAF officer to decide exactly who was responsible for bringing down each plane or bug, whether naval guns, RAF or AA guns. In some cases, a kill would be divided between two of the services which resulted in half a swastika each. Of the 9,000 divers which fell in Britain, killing 6,584 people, one fell at Bygrave, 107 in Hertfordshire.

After experimenting with a giant rocket in the first years of the war, the German scientist, Werner von Braun, tested it out in 1942 but fortunately for us and the world it was not perfected until 1944, when it became Hitler's second secret weapon, the V2.

The first V2, 46' long, 5'6" in diameter, containing a ton of explosives and weighing about 15 tons with a range of about 200 miles, travelling at a previously unheard of speed of 3,000 miles per hour, fell at Chiswick on 8 September at 1900 hours, killing two people and injuring ten more. Goebbels, Head of Nazi Propaganda, said this would force England to her knees.

From Trimley we saw the vivid flash as a V2 was being launched over there in Holland. Between September 1944 and April 1945 1,120 were launched against Britain and 1,120 fell here, 47 in Hertfordshire.

But the end of the war against Germany and its European Allies was coming to a rapid end and at the end of April 1945, Hitler had committed suicide and Ashwellians were able quietly to celebrate victory in Europe. A Children's Sports Day was held on the Recreation Ground on 8 May. Refreshments were provided by the three bakers, Charles Day, George Morley and Sid Lindsay of Guilden Morden, while the loudspeaker van for music and announcements was loaned by William Reeves.

It was not until August that year, after two Atomic Bombs had been dropped in Japan, effectively ending the war in the Pacific that Ashwell really celebrated as the closing account from the Herts Express newspaper (25/8/1945) describes:'

"Scenes such as had never before been witnessed at Ashwell took place on VJ celebration night, when practically the whole community gathered in the old market square for a street dance. The dancers' ages ranged from 7 to 70. Music was provided by a loudspeaker and the scene was brilliantly lit from the decorations outside Tommy Dennis's shop, augmented by the street lamps, which were switched on for the first time for six years. Dancing continued until the early hours of the morning. On the Wednesday evening, as darkness fell, a huge bonfire was lit in the meadow on the high ground towards Bygrave Road. There was also a fireworks display.

On Thursday afternoon a programme of sports was carried through on the Recreation Ground and tea, lemonade and cakes were served to everyone. A dance was held in the Village Hall in the evening, a small charge was made so that the Homecoming Fund might benefit. This continued until midnight when the dancers adjourned to the street dance. The Hall dance, the collection at the street dance, a competition for vegetables and voluntary donations from these brought in altogether £30 for the Homecoming fund. There were no incidents of damage or injury during the celebrations, the whole effect being one of spontaneous happiness. The celebrations were inaugurated at a public meeting called by the Parish Council and held only a few hours before the official peace announcement was received.

During the war, dances, whist drives and other events had been held to provide a Homecoming Fund. This finally amounted to £800 and was shared between Ashwell members of the forces. I received a £7.00 cheque, to which I added ten shillings and bought a stick-type barometer.

As the men and women returned from the forces, there was plenty of work to be found at Baldock where the Kayser Bondor factory was turning over to a new product, nylon stockings, and at Letchworth the factories were switching over to peace time production. Kryn and Lahey, part of the George Cohen group of companies, went from the production of bomb and shell cases to heavy castings for railway engines and other equipment and later on to cranes. Shelvoke and Drury's motorised dust carts were soon to be found in most countries. The Spirella factory changed from corsets to all kinds of ladies' underwear. Marmet prams were now called baby carriages. Dents, the well-known publishers, expanded and Meredews continued making quality furniture. Makers of Sellotape and small engineering works all needed workers.

In the early 1950s, Borg Warner set up a large factory in Jubilee Road to make automatic transmission gear, employing about 1,000 people and just across the road Armco tube manufacturers employed another 500 or so.

Many of these workers came from the surrounding towns and villages - Royston, the Mordens and Ashwell from our direction.

When the US Army Airforce left Steeple Morden and Bassingbourn, a few taking brides with them (known as GI brides) and some leaving babies behind, the farmers set to work breaking up the concrete runways to reclaim their land, when quite out of the blue came the rumour that the newly appointed New Towns Commission was looking at this as the site of Britain's first new town, to house thousands of people.

Eventually, it was said, the town could spread from Royston almost to Baldock, swallowing everything in its path.

There was great relief among the farming community, when the Commissioners decided that it would be wiser to build the new town alongside a main line railway nearer to London, and so Stevenage had the honour of becoming the first of Britain's new towns.

Ashwell people who served in the war

The list of those who served in the Second World War has been compiled by Philip Crump, long-serving Chairman of the Ashwell Branch of the British Legion, who has studied the fading Roll of Honour, now stored in the Museum. Philip believes that this was originally compiled by Geoffrey C Whitby, Headmaster of Merchant Taylors' School. Two names were rather faded but he hopes he has copied them correctly. As far as possible, the Service in which they served has been given, but rank and decorations have been omitted as so much of this information is incomplete.

Roll of Honour
Names of those from Ashwell on active service for King and Country 1939-1945

Roy Ablett RASC

Kenneth Arthur Andrews RAOC

Geoffrey Arthur Herts & Beds Regt

William (Senr) Barnes RN HMS Flora

Arthur G Baulk RAF

Cyril Bean RAOC

Benedict Beresford Royal Marines

Morris Bird Wiltshire Regt

John M Bray RA

Kenneth Bryant RAF Medical Corps

Ernest A Bullard Herts & Beds Regt

Bernard Bullen Regimental Police

Kenneth C Bullock RAF

C Hope Carlton Army Medical Service

Sydney Cheetham RAF Trans REME

Anthony Christy RAF

ohn Christy RAFVR

Robert Christy RA Signals

Georgina W M Clements RA ?? ATS

John Collins RASC

Edward O Critchley East African AMC

Kenneth Crump RAF

Ronald John Daniels 7th Herts & Beds

Reginald John Davies RASC

Howard Edwin Day Fleet Air Arm RN

Edward Eversden Royal Marines

Gordon Francis Recce Corps

Lawrence H Gallant RA

Ernest Gaunt RAF

Bernard Hankin Herts & Beds Regt

John Harradine RA

Anthony Eustace Hill RAF VR

Neville John Howes RAF

Frederick Izzard RA

Ivy D James ATS 1st LAA Regt RA

Dermot Thomas Kearney RASC

James Law Royal Marines

Charles Gordon Levitt Gloucestershire Regt

John Mander Welsh Fusiliers

John Talbot Marsden AIF

Stanley Alfred Marshall RN HMS Cossack

John Moss RAF

Anthony Oyston Royal Tank Corps

Frederick Chas Page Beds & Herts

Percy Pammenter RASC

Albert Parrish RASC

Leo Pickett Herts & Beds Regt

Julian Raikes RHA

Lancelot G Rawlins RAF VR

Percy Revels RASC

Charles Revill RAF

George William Revils RA

Ronald Robins RAF

Rodney Rowland RA

Hubert Ryland RE

Neville Albon RN

William Henry Appleton RAF

William T (Jnr) Barnes RNAS (Photographer)

Wilfred E Barrow RAF VR

Robin Beadle Royal Corps Signals

William Bean Royal Marines

John Christopher Beresford Royal Norfolk Regt

Roy Bonnet RFA Beds & Herts Territorials RA

William Henry Bromley Pioneer Corps

Lawrence Bryant RAF VR

Harry Arthur Bullard Army (Regt not shown)

Philip Bulley Hants Regt

Ernest Carey RN

John Chaffey Army

Stanley Cherry RASC

Beatrice Mary Christy WAAF

Neville Edwin Christy RAF

Christopher Clements RN

Mary Clements RAMC ATS

Robert Crack RN HMS Queensworth

Bob Crump RFA Beds & Herts Territorials RA

Philip Crump Irish Guards

John Henry Davies RA

Robert Davies Herts & Beds & RMP

Frank Duffy RN Harold Victor Eley RAF

Keith Eversden Beds & Herts Reg

Dorothy Furr ATS Elsie Furr WRNS

Alec John Game Pioneer Corps

William Herbert Geeves RASC

Ernest Hankin RN A

Bramwell Harvey RAF

Julian Eustace Hill RAF VR

William Herbert Huffer Recce Corps

Elsie A James ATS 1st LAA Regt RA

William James RAF

Derrick Philip Kingsley RASC

N Lawman Manageress NAAFI

Edward A Thomas Mack RAF VR

Barbara Marsden WAAF

Kenneth Marsden RAF

Kenneth Harvey Miller Beds & Herts Regt

Frederick Moule Signals Corps

Charles A Page RA

George A Page RASC

Reay Parkinson RN

William Pettengell Beds & Herts Territorials RA

Alan Picking RA

Rienard Raikes QVR

Kenneth Revels RN

Stanley Revels RN

Stanley Albert Revill Queens Royal Regt

Sidney Reynolds Herts & Beds Regt

Elizabeth Rose WAAF

Dorothy Jean Rumbold WAAF

Albert Sheldrick RA

Sybil Sheldrick ATS
Bernard Simmons RAC
Thomas Herbert Skerman Royal Marines
Douglas Smyth RA
Sheila Titcombe WAAF
Harold Waldock RA
Clifford Redvers Ward RA
Arthur Webb MIL Pioneer Corps
John A Whitby RN
Eric White RN
Russell Percival White RA
William Whitehead RA
Alan Willatts RN
Frank Willatts RN
William H Wiltshire RAF
Eric Worboys Durham Light Infantry
Stanley Worboys RASC
 Peter Wright RAF

Dan Gurney Sheppard Herts & Beds Regt
Frank W Skerman RAF
Thomas F Smith RASC
Vera Strickland Land Army
Douglas Waldock 1st Herts Regt
Edmund G Wallis RA
Redvers H Ward RE
Ernest Westerman RA
Edward White Herts & Beds Regt
Horace White RASC
Stanley Whitehead RA
Frederick Wilkins RE
Henry F Willatts RN
Alec Williamson RAMC
Bryan Worboys RASC
Harold William Worboys RA
Theo Worboys RASC
Tom John Wylie Norfolk Regt

The names of the following Ashwell men who failed to return were chiselled on the base of the war memorial: William Bean Kenneth Eversden Anthony Eustace Hill James Law Stanley Marshall George Page William Pettengell Richard Raikes Douglas Waldock

420,000 British Sailors, Soldiers and Airmen and 30,000 British Merchant Seaman died in the Second World War. 60,000 Civilians were killed in air raids on Britain, and 86000 were badly injured.

After the war, many Ashwellians served in the Armed Forces, doing their "National Service", which did not end until 31 December 1960. These are listed below. Again, Philip has been to a great deal of trouble to compile it.

John Anderson RAF
John Bonnett Army
Fred Bryant Army
Tony Bullock RAF
Peter Chamberlain Army
Peter Cherry (Green Lane) Army
Mick Dilley RAF
Gordon Gentle RN
Norman Gurney RAF
Peter Howes RAF
David Lambert RAF
Henry Livings RAF
Peter Moynihan RAF
Leon Picking RAF
Mick Revels Army
Noel Sheldrick RAF
Johnie Sheppard Army
David Tweed RN
John Westrope Army
Don Willats RAF

John Barton Army
Ron Bowen Army
Peter Bryant Army
Doug Chaffey Army
Dick Cherry RN
Terry Crump Army
Tony Eley Army
Pearl Glasscock RAF
Octavious Hammond RAF
Roger Howes RAF
Eric Levitt RAF
Derek Marshal Army
Mick Oyston RAF
Tony Picking Army
David Seaby RAF
Robert Sheldrick Army
Ray Skerman Army
Fred Ward RAF
Martin Whitby RAF
Bill Worboys Army

David Blagg RAF
Bob Brown Army
Roger Bryant RAF
Vic Chaffey Army
Peter Cherry Army
Bill Davies Army
Gerald Gallant RAF
Eric Gurney RAF
Peter Hankin Army
John Kearney RAF
Reg Levitt RN
John Mathews Army
Jim Peters RAF
Margaret Reeves WRENS
Nick Sheldrick Army
Gurney Sheppard Army
Richard Stafford Army
Bryan Walters RAF
Peter Whitby RAF
Rod Worboys RN

Ashwell at School

It was all change in the education of Ashwell's children in 1933. Until then, the girls, after attending the mixed Infants School from 5-7, were transferred to the Girls' School next door, under Miss Anne Hyslop until they reached the age of 14. The boys went to the Merchant Taylors' School also till 14, when their formal education ended. A few, however, were able enough to obtain a scholarship or by paying a fee, to go to one of the Grammar Schools elsewhere.

In 1933, the old Board School became a Primary Mixed School with all pupils staying until 11, with Miss Hyslop in charge. The Merchant Taylors' became a Senior Mixed School, 11-14 year olds, to which Mr Geoffrey Whitby had recently been appointed Headmaster.

Howard Day, who was born in 1922, recalls that when he attended the Infants' School at the age of five, Miss Anne Hyslop was Head Teacher and Miss Annie Bray was her assistant, while Miss Ida Graves taught the infant boys.

Howard said,

> "We were taught to write letters and numbers with chalk on our slates, and to sew a button on a piece of cloth. Later we used pencils when we were taught the three Rs.
>
> "There were no school dinners, the children from Newnham and Hinxworth brought sandwiches and those who lived in Ashwell went home for the midday meal. We collected frogs spawn and watched it turn into tadpoles.
>
> "Periodically the district nurse came to look for body lice in our hair, with two meat skewers and some antiseptic. My grandfather was very annoyed as he thought I was clean enough. The lavatories were outside and very cold in winter.
>
> "When we were eleven we went back to the Merchant Taylors' School which had just been changed to a mixed school - a complete new system, with Mr G C Whitby the first Headmaster."

Some children, as before 1933, could make it to the Grammar Schools at Letchworth and Hitchin. For example, Norman Gurney managed to get to Hitchin by passing an entrance examination, but his parents had to pay £5 0s 0d a term as he was not good enough academically to get a scholarship. In fact, the first pupil for many years to win a scholarship was Dorothy Brown in 1940 and a year later Peter Howes achieved the same distinction.

Miss Hyslop retired in 1941, after 24 years, and was succeeded by James Dunkerley, already well known in the village as the evacuee Headmaster who had come to Ashwell with his schoolchildren in 1939. After he retired in 1945, Miss D C Reddall, former Head of Newnham Church of England School which, together with Hinxworth School, was closed, succeeded him, retiring in 1949.

In the meantime, the Merchant Taylors' School was closed in 1947, its pupils being transferred mainly to Knights Templar, Baldock. Later, many Ashwell pupils went to the Royston schools of Greneway and Meridian.

Back to Ashwell's Primary School: Mr R Norris was Headmaster for only 16 months being succeeded in 1950 by Tom Pryor, a very popular man, Parish Councillor for a time, Museum Trustee, singer with the Church Choir, thoroughly integrating into Ashwell's life.

Pupils of the Infant School, 1926. With their teacher Miss Annie Bray. Back Row L to R: *Not Known, Not Known, Eileen White, Gwen Tyler, Eadie Game, Nelly Revels, Mona Mitchell, Joan Collins, Miss Annie Bray.* Middle Row: *Bill James, Ken Andrews, Jim Law, Cyril Worboys Not Known, Eadie Davis, Vera Strickland.* Front: *Bill Huffer, Alan Picking, Derrick Tyler, Cliff Ward, Frank Duffy, Ken Crump, Frank Skerman . (Alan Picking)*

Merchant Taylors' School Boys, 1930. Back L to R: *John Revels, Dennis Morley, ? Bradfield, Cliff Ward, Frank Duffy, Geoffrey Arthurs, Frank skerman.* Middle: *Cyril Worboys, Alan Picking, David Christy, Kenneth Crump, William Huffer, James Law, Derek Tyler, Teacher Miss Gwen Biles.* Front: *William James, ? Clements, ? Horsley, Arnold Grey, Bob Crump, N. John Howes, Ken Andrews, Unknown. (Peter Howes)*

Children at Ashwell School c.1950.
Back Row L to R: *David Cherry, Basil Bryant, John Simmons.* 2nd Row: *Edward Booker, Robert Chandler, Barbara Gifford, Robina Stuckley, Valerie McBeale, Marion Geeves, Carol Francis, Robert Rosendale, Colin Sackett.* 3rd Row: *John Clements, Martin McBeale, Joyce Waldock, Pat Dellar, Jessica Kanella, Headmaster Tom Pryor, Betty Brown, Rosalind Brown, Ann Bullard, Ronnie Hayes.* Front: *Michael Chandler, John Foster, Scott the dog, Barry Pinker, Colin Brown.* (May Cook)
Below: 1953. Back Row L to R: *Roger Rowland, Anthony Tweed, Albert Livings, Trevor Mitchell, Colin Sackett, Rodney Leete* Second Row: *Mary Bonnett, Ruth Gallant, Mary Lavelle, Edith Webster, Jill Izzard, Jennifer Clarke, Mary Haylock, Ann Huffer, Monica Horne, Carol Chandler.* Seated: *John Foster, Sonia Capon, Ruth Everett, Maureen Moule, Rachel Gurney, John Wheeler Teacher, Sheila Wilkins, Christine Chapman, Linda Raven, Jackie Hoye, Barry Newman.* Bottom Row: *John Norman, Jean Auburn, Reggie Powell.* (Mary Haylock)

During the 2nd World War pigs and sheep were kept at the Merchant Taylors' School, and its pupils taught to look after them.

1940's: Evacuee children with their headmaster James Dunkerley (top right) and other teachers. (Museum)

The School Band (1938-39). L to R: Bill Davies, Mary Anderson, Dorothy Brown, Beryl Wilkins, Olive Day, Roger Howes, Mary Day, Margaret Reeves, Roy Worboys, Terry Crump, Peggy Gallant, Peter Howe, Margaret Worboys, George Worboys (Nora Reeves)

But he was not popular with all his pupils. Mary Haylock relates that because she was unable to do long division he would slap her round the back of her legs with a ruler. To protect herself, she stuffed exercise books down her socks! What is, however, beyond question, the education received at the Primary School was excellent of its type and you left with a thorough grounding in the 3 Rs, and mostly with fond memories of a happy childhood education. The teachers were highly respected and most took a very active part in village activities, so there was plenty of interaction between the school and the parents and the rest of the village. The system of education was in any case run on well established formal principles and unlike the turmoil of the past thirty odd years, all knew what to expect and the standards the pupils, all but the dullest, were expected to attain.

In 1971, Tom Pryor resigned because of ill health to be succeeded by John Bushell, who was Headmaster until 1977. During these two Headships, there were two major building developments, the first in 1957, which enabled all the pupils to come together under one roof. Because of space problems, the school canteen had to be in the Village Hall, and two classes had to be accommodated in the Further Education Centre. With a new Hall, new classrooms, inside toilets, and a small staff room, the school was in much better shape. By 1974, the old school house had been demolished and a new more spacious Assembly Hall had been built, providing not only improvements for the pupils but additional facilities for other village organisations.

Meanwhile, the Parent Teachers Association, started in the early 60s, had really got into gear, deciding in 1971 to fund an outside swimming pool project which cost over £5000 and was officially opened in June 1975 with a splash - Headmaster, John Bushell and PTA Chairman, Rod Leete being thrown in at the opening ceremony. The PTA has continued to play a very active part in the progress of the school.

Although 1947 saw the end of the Merchant Taylors' School - its number of pupils had declined to just over 30 - its first Headmaster after it became a Mixed School in 1933 brought new practices and a broader outlook. Geoffrey Whitby was a man of many talents apart from his teaching abilities - musician, craftsman, expert gardener, among other attributes. He organised at Ashwell an experimental programme, with emphasis on rural studies, including agriculture and natural history, and on handicrafts. His wife, Mabel, also a trained teacher, was assistant mistress and a great support. An outside theatre was built and a school orchestra organised very successfully. During the war, the school population was considerably increased by evacuees, and with wartime shortages a small flock of sheep and goats were acquired, and additionally some allotments, tended by the children, the produce being used for school meals or distributed to the children. Mrs Mabel Whitby was the Head of Merchant Taylors' for a short time after the war - her husband having become Herts County Organiser for Rural Education - and when the school closed down she became the first Warden of the Adult Education Centre, which continued under her guidance until 1967, when Mrs Dena Lewis took over. Records for the Centre are rather scant but in the early days various evening classes were held - art classes led by Mary Hoad, who stimulated the generation of Ashwell artists

The Merchant Taylors School closed in 1947. Then became The Further Education Centre, and the Library originally housed at the Village Hall moved in.
Seated: *Joyce Andrews and Mrs. Pidgeon with h er daughter Marilyn, Miss L. Cooper (with hat) standing. Librarians seated: Mrs. M. Seymour and Mrs. I. Bowman. The portrait is that of Sir William Gentle. (David Short)*

Ashwell Primary School Kitchen and Dining Hall Staff.
Back row: *Sadie Davis, Eileen Peacock, Carol Moore, Elsie Powell.*
Front: *Sheila Swallow, Jean Collins, Joan Ball, Rose Simmons, Pat Hankin. 1970's*
(Alan Picking)

which followed; pottery classes were held in what was then known as the Technical Room - woodworking, music, drama, dressmaking were among other classes. The Infant Welfare Clinic from 1947 was held fortnightly and operated until the new surgery was built in Gardiners Lane. The Library was moved from the Village Hall to the Centre that year and open Tuesday afternoons and Wednesday evenings. Mrs Lewis's husband, David, was in charge of the first Field Studies Courses, which came into being in 1968. So the pioneering work of the Whitbys in rural environmental education was maintained and indeed extended. Field Studies help to enhance the textbook information on environmental matters and themselves stimulate the further pursuit of environmental knowledge from practical observation.

At the end of our period, Dena Lewis was replaced by David Short and, in 1977, Lis Short became Warden with David as Advisory Teacher and his responsibilities were for the first time broadened beyond Ashwell.

In 1993, the future of the Centre has become somewhat uncertain, but the potential is challenging and exciting.

In the formative years of the Centre, Ashwell was the home of John Newsom, the Herts County Education Officer from 1940 to 1957. He and his wife, Barbara, an active participant in Ashwell affairs, including a spell as a Parish Councillor, lived in Bear House from 1946 to 1957. Mr Newsom (later Sir John Newsom), a man of many ideas, was a good supporter of the Centre, seeing it as an enterprise similar to the village colleges being set up in Cambridgeshire.

Memories of the old Merchant Taylors' School were revived by one of the most colourful events Ashwell has witnessed this century.

On Saturday, 29 May 1976, five of the Wardens of the Worshipful Company of Merchant Taylors bedecked in their ermine-edged gowns and Tudor hats rode into the village on Sam Wallace's Hay Wagon, pulled by eight strong young men and preceded by a drum and a band of children playing "Greensleeves" on their recorders, followed by a procession of residents including the members of the Merchant Taylors' Further Education Committee.

The street, lined with people in Victorian dress, were bedecked with Union Jacks and banners, one bearing the words 'God Save the Queen'. The crowds cheered when the wagon pulled up at the Three Tuns, where the landlord was waiting with eight glasses of beer for the eight young men. The procession then moved on until it reached the Museum, where on a platform erected for the occasion, the chairman of the day, the late Eric Harradine, an old boy of the School, gave an address of welcome to the wardens and thanked them for coming once again to Ashwell.

Then followed the presentation of souvenirs to the Wardens by children whose ancestors were at school in 1876. After photographs had been taken the party moved on to the school, now the Ashwell Further Education Centre, where an exhibition had been laid on.

This very successful event was organised to celebrate the centenary of the re-opening of the school on 26 May 1876 after the building of the main classroom. On that occasion, the Master and Wardens had travelled by express train from London. The train was stopped at Ashwell, where they had been met by a wagonette. On arrival at Lucas Lane, the horses were replaced by eight young

The Celebrations on 29th May 1976 the Centenary of the opening of Merchant Taylors' School.
Above: *Eight strong men, each fortified by a glass of beer at the Three Tuns, draw the Wagon of Merchant Taylors' visitors along the High Street.* (David Short)

Bottom Left: *In period dress the people of Ashwell follow.* (David Short)

Bottom Right: *Gathering at the Museum for an official welcome from Eric Harradine, an old boy of the school.* (Photograph by Stan Ackroyd/Museum)

men who pulled the wagonette into the village through decorated streets and under ivy-covered arches. On arrival at Market hill they were met by Mr E K Fordham, Chairman of the School Board.

After the Wardens had inspected the new classroom, the pupils were given a new shilling each and a half day's holiday, while the guests adjourned to the rectory for lunch. Pictures of this auspicious day can be seen in Ashwell Museum.

More Centenary celebrations

Ashwell School went all Victorian, when the staff and 173 pupils celebrated the school's 100th anniversary on the last day of February, 1978.

The actual anniversary was on 8 April but due to the Easter holiday the celebrations were held earlier.

The Headmaster, Mr Greville Pugh, (1977-1983) wearing a gown and mortar board and with a cane at the ready, kept the pupils in order. The rest of the staff, ladies wearing frilled bustle dresses and the men in tails and bat wing collars hired from Richard Rosendale of Newnham, little girls in pinafores and mob caps, the boys wearing short trousers, waistcoats and caps lined up in the playground before going into school for assembly, when they all stood while readings were given from the Bible, and good old Victorian hymns were sung.

Such mottoes as 'Spare the rod and spoil the child' and 'Love thy neighbour' appeared on the walls and the teaching was definitely 'Reading, Riting and Rithmatic'. At playtime one of the boys rang a handbell and again at the end.

After grace had been said the children sat down to a meal of stew, potatoes and cabbage with ground rice pudding for afters, cooked by Mrs Joan Ball and her assistants and served by the dinner ladies wearing mob caps and pinafores. Both Mrs Ball and Alan Picking, then caretaker, were pupils at the school some fifty years earlier. Mr Pugh said that when the school opened, Miss Gwillam was the first teacher, with 96 children attending school for the first time.

Ashwell photographer, Stan Ackroyd, wearing a deerstalker hat and Norfolk jacket, took photographs of the staff and pupils in the playground.

A special service to celebrate the Centenary was held at the Parish Church. A week later a grand reunion of over 80 old pupils was held at the school including 91 year old Annie Chapman who was a pupil at the school during the 1890s and later one of its longest-serving teachers. Painstakingly, Mr Pugh had searched the early registers and given each of the old pupils a badge with their name and the years when they had attended the school. Over half of these were still living in Ashwell.

Mr and the Hon Mrs Jeremy Fordham were present at the gathering. They provided the refreshments, as had their ancestors Mr and Mrs Edward King Fordham at the School's opening a century earlier.

Ashwell School Centenary, 1978. *Photograph of staff and children in period costume.*
In doorway: *Joan Ball, Jean Collins, Sheila Swallow, Myra Duffy, Eileen Holloway.*
On left: *Sandra Holloway, Pat Nightingale, Greville Pugh (Headmaster), Joan Bath, Maggie Taylor.*
On right: *John Berrett, Diane Churchill, Helen Slater.*
(Photograph by Stan Ackroyd/Alan Picking School Caretaker)

A view from the school meadow, the Head Teacher's house and garden to the left. Demolished to make way for the new Assembly Hall, built in 1973. (Museum)

Ashwell at Work

On the Farms (NJG)

The farmer by Jack Catterick May 1955

Fifty years anon
In a past that's long gone
I had six horses,
ewe lambs by the score,
with cows and pigs,
and more -
merry men, who drank Harvest ale
brown or pale.
Now inside my farm there's not a cat
upon the mat
nor e'er a rat
nor a mouse
within the house.
(For we have a rodent officer who come
each fourteen days to drive them from their homes
and an official - some big nob -
to see they do their job.)

But I have tractors three
(though a tractor is no companion)
A combine, a thresher and a drum
how I love to hear them hum -
Their whine is music to my ear;
With them, and subsidies, I've nought to fear.

Inside my cowshed now I pack
Fison's and Bibbys by the sack;
potash and bonemeal, brown permanganate,
and death to the weeds, sodium chlorate.
The travellers are always at my gate
with some new thing I trow.
(God knows what men are eating now.)
My sheds are full, and I must build before
the winter comes, to store
things to make the soil yield even more;
for I must produce - by Big Brother it is said -
he is God - the executive his rod.
He is my Lord, now there is no squire,
sand in the village church no choir.
I barter piece terms with my men,
and then there is no peace
but argument and discontent
with union rates not broken gates.
Diesel for milk
plastic for silk
such is the morn
that now is born
and with it I must cast my lot
- or rot.

The Rev Jack Catterick's somewhat satirical poem on the role of the farmer reflects the transition from farming by horse and man to mechanised husbandry.

In 1939, although the tractor was well used, there were plenty of farms which relied on the horse to pull the plough, the reaper, the seed drills, etc and, in 1946, it was still quite a normal occurrence for the harvest to be gathered in by traditional methods. First the reaper cut the corn and bundled it into sheaves. These were stacked, usually in groups of eight, so that they were properly dried in the sun. When ready, the willing horse pulling the cart waited patiently by each shock as it was picked up by pitchfork and put into the cart. Eventually a full load, very carefully loaded, was taken to a corner of the field where it was either off loaded on to an elevator and erected into a stack to be thrashed later or processed through a thrashing machine, which was driven by a steam engine. The surplus straw was made into stacks. These laborious procedures required a lot of workers and often schoolboys on holiday could earn a few 'bob' helping out at the farm.

The combine harvester and other advanced machinery was to change all this after the Second World War.

John Sale and Sam Wallace of Farrows Farm

Tenant farmer, John Sale, died in 1896. In his last will and testament he asked his executors, farmer Cooper of Dixies Farm and farmer Wright of Bear Farm to keep an eye on and advise his sixteen year old son, John Sale, who took over the tenancy of Farrows Farm.

In 1919, John Sale bought the farm for £6,000. During the twenties and early thirties a recession and a world wide downward turn in trade hit farming seriously and when the farm was valued in the late twenties it was not worth £3,000.

Strange as it may seem, it was Hitler, the dictator, and the Daily Mail who saved the British farmers' bacon. Hitler stabilised grain prices in Germany by ensuring that every farmer got at least an agreed minimum price for his produce, and in 1934/35 after the Daily Mail had run a campaign, the government gave in and agreed to follow Hitler's policy. And so John Sale wrote in huge letters of mustard on Belly Hill, off Newnham Road, 'THANK YOU DAILY MAIL'.

An Australian named Edwards was at Dunton Lodge Farm during the war and it was he who introduced the first combine harvester to this area in about 1939, and according to Mrs Mack, the Angells were the first Ashwell farmers to have this machine.

John Sale and his son-in-law were not impressed with earlier models as so much grain was left on the straw and on the ground. By 1947 the mechanics of the combine harvester had greatly improved and Bill Wallace ordered one (self propelled) for Bluegates Farm and not to be outdone his father-in-law, John Sale, also ordered one (tractor drawn) for Farrows Farm.

At the outbreak of war in 1939, Ashwell's farmers had wondered how they would be affected? How many of their workers would they lose to the armed forces? Would the supply of fertilisers dry up and how would the war affect their supplies of petrol and diesel oil to fuel the tractors and other machines? The government, remembering the submarine menace of the First World War, set up a Ministry of Food, headed by Lord Woolton, with a War Agricultural Committee in each area to advise, to watch slack farmers, to ensure that unused land was brought into cultivation and that all land was used to its full capacity.

The slogan, 'Dig for Victory' was not only for gardeners. Fuel rationing was brought in and to give farmers more hours of daylight, Double Summer time was introduced.

John Sale remembered not only the First World War when the army commandeered some of his horses, but the Boer War as well. He carried on farming his 300+ acres up and over Newnham Hill, growing barley, oats, wheat and peas. During the 1920s he had a range of piggeries built, but after so many of the pigs died he gave up, blaming the cold concrete floors.

Sam Wallace, at the age of 21, joined his grandfather as a partner in 1963, when the farm employed three workers, Albert Harradine, Basil Worboys and Ben Game. In 1967, Sam once again introduced pigs to the farm. For the next 15 years productivity increased considerably, not only with the pig herd but also because new varieties of wheat, together with better chemicals weed control, increased yields. Further understanding of pests and diseases of cereal crops and the introduction of fungicides and insecticides to control them also enhanced yields.

Top: *Once upon a time corn was cut by men with scythes and tied up by hand. Then came the Massey Harris self-binder, drawn by horses. 1930's.* (Gurney Sheppard)
Below: *After World War II, Massey Ferguson produced the Combine Harvester seen here with Bert Brown on the platform, Albert Brown (Geordie) and farmer Maurice Brown of Dixies Farm. 1960's.* (Mrs. E. Brown)
Left: *Aerial spraying was a common sight until the late 70's. Later, tractors were designed to carry spraying attachments which were more accurate.* (Gurney Sheppard)

The government, with subsidies for buildings, fertilisers and weed killers, encouraged farmers to grow as much food as possible and thus avoid the high cost of imports. But we were still not growing enough wheat to feed Britain until the late seventies when production increased and by the early 1980s we became self-sufficient and at the same time the 'Bakery Research Institute' had found ways of using greater quantities of British wheat instead of the more usual Canadian hard wheat. Today so much wheat is grown that we export between two and three million tonnes annually.

John Sale died in 1972, aged 94. The oak gates at the Church Lane entrance to the churchyard were erected to his memory.

Westbury Farm

Benjamin Christy had been farming at Westbury Farm, with the help of his mother, since leaving the Merchant Taylors' School in 1876, aged 14. So by the year 1939 Benjamin was prepared to hand over the running of the farm to his younger son, Raymond, then aged 20.

Ray Christy worked hard, growing wheat, barley, oats, brussels and sugar beet on the land behind the Village Hall down to Park Lane and over the other side of Hinxworth road, from West Point over Quarry Hill to the Caldecote boundary. At the farm yard he fattened some beef cattle.

A small brass plate, screwed to the Lych Gate, states that it was repaired and re-tiled in memory of Benjamin Christy, who died in 1949, aged 87.

Ray Christy carried on farming, modernised the farm buildings, used the latest fertilisers to increase the grain yield and sprayed weed killers, to kill off the scarlet poppies and yellow charlocks which had always given Quarry Hill field that look of a Manet painting, but at the same time had ruined the grain samples.

Raymond Christy was taken ill and died in 1965, aged 46. His death, the family believe, was caused by the weed killer.

Westbury Farm was bought in 1966 by the Jeremy Fordham Farming Partnership and barley, wheat, peas and beans are still grown. The farm buildings have been replaced by well designed dwellings built in the same style as the original farm buildings.

Dixies Farm

Tenant farmer, Frank Brown, came to Dixies Farm with his wife, two sons and daughter in 1930. While Maurice, the elder son, worked the land, Geoffrey, the younger son, looked after the dairy side, until one night in 1942 he was killed in a motor cycle accident.

Soon after the war Frank retired, Dixies Farmhouse was divided into two properties and Maurice took over the farm and ran it until he was taken ill in 1972. The Farr family of Newnham, the owners of the farm, then took over the 350 acres of land, which is mainly over Claybush Hill, and continued to grow wheat, barley, peas, potatoes, oil seed rape and sugar beet, all worked from their Newnham farm. Dixies Farmhouse was sold and the farm buildings which were no longer needed were also sold to developers in 1978 who, it was said, while preserving the barns hoped to provide work opportunities for local people and to prevent Ashwell from becoming simply a commuter area.

In Back Street the old cart shed had been taken down and in 1976 eight houses were built with reclaimed bricks in a little mews called the Rickyard.

Bear Farm

Bear Farm was in 1889 part of the 1,500 acre estate of Edward King Fordham, whose grandson, Oswald, sold the farm to the Farr family of Newnham about 1930.

They farmed the land on the Kingsland road and sold Bear House, which after a number of owners, is now in the possession of the Colquhoun family.

The farm buildings were sold to the Ashwell Housing Association in 1978, whose idea it was to convert those on Short Bear Lane into bungalows and to build houses to let to Ashwell people in Back Street.

Whitby Farm

The Angell family owns Whitby Farm and the house next door to the Village Tea Rooms. In the early 1970s, the Angells sold their Silver Street meadow for a quarter of a million pounds, and 44 houses were built there between 1975 and 1978.

Mrs Kathleen Mack, one of the two Angell sisters (the other Christine), was one of the instigators of the revived Ashwell Horse Show which took place for the first time after the Second World War in 1948.

The farmyard then was an immaculate array of buildings and stables. Mrs Mack was a skilled horsewoman, who was largely responsible for establishing the high standards of the Show Jumping and events involving horses at the Ashwell Show.

The farm itself, stretching from the Newnham Road, taking in Arbury Banks, over to the Bygrave Road, had about 300 acres, and cultivated arable crops. Since the death from cancer of the hardworking Christine, who laboured until her demise in 1991, the farm has been run solely by her brother, Gerald Angell, and most of the land in 1993 is "set aside".

Redlands Farm

The 370 acre Redlands Farm on the Station road, at one time part of Sir George Fordham's Odsey estate, was sold by Sir George's son, Willie Herbert, to the Northern family in the 1930s.

When, in the 1960s, drilling for oil took place at Redlands Farm, Willie Herbert, an authority on oil, said it was the last place he would expect to find oil. Nor did they.

Redlands is a mixed farm with pigs and beef cattle; peas, potatoes, cereals and oil seed are grown. As a matter of interest, the growing of oil seed rape would appear to be something new in this area, but it was grown in Ashwell in the 1840s. The day after the great fire of Ashwell in 1850, the village was visited by hundreds of people from the surrounding area to see the devastation. Harry Cannon, a Hitchin confectioner, was one of the sightseers and, as a souvenir from one of the burned barns, picked up a chunk of charred grain and another of charred rape seed, both of which Harry's son presented to Ashwell Museum.

Ashridge Farm

By the age of 9, Eric Gurney was one of those lucky boys who knew exactly what he wanted to be - a farmer. Eric spent all of his spare time at Dixies Farm, feeding and mucking out the pigs and cattle, learning the art of farming from Maurice Brown, and attending the Ashwell Farmers' Discussion Group. It took him twenty years to achieve his dream.

While still very young, Eric married Audrey Pidgeon in 1950 and they raised their family very early. During the early 1960s the young couple ran Ashwell Stores, very efficiently, probably while waiting for a suitable farm to become available and when it did they called it Ashridge Farm.

Ashridge Farm has only appeared on the map since 1964.

The 130 acre farm was made up of fields off the Ruddery, Ashwell Street, where the modern farm house and farm buildings are. Some of the small fields of which the farm is made up only appeared after the enclosure award of 1863, when they were awarded to cottagers in lieu of their rights to graze sheep and cattle on the common lands. The field behind the Old Maltings building was for many years divided into allotments and owned by Fordham's Brewery.

Ashridge Farm currently produces potatoes, beans and cereals.

Entrepreneurial Eric, wife Audrey and son Stuart have diversified, like so many small farmers, into making different use of their land apart from food production. For some years to the present time, a log supply business is also run alongside a Caravan Rally Site which has been very successful. Further expansion is planned including the provision of improved facilities.

Bluegates Farm

William Hamilton Wallace first came to Ashwell in the 1920s to manage the thousand acres of the combined Bluegates and Ducklake Farms for Mrs Phyllis Fordham; his marriage to Bessie, the daughter of Mr and Mrs John Sale of Farrows Farm followed. At Bluegates Farmhouse they raised their family of two sons and four daughters, and at the same time grew cereals, sugar beet, potatoes, maize and kale to feed the Bluegates Dairy Herd.

After the death of Mrs Fordham in 1958 he carried on farming for another ten years when, in 1968, Mrs Fordham's great-nephew, the young Michael Gurney Sheppard, came into the Bury estate, and the Wallaces left Bluegates Farmhouse and moved into their newly built house called 'Sales Acre', a stone's throw away from Farrows Farm, where Bessie was born. Bill Wallace died in 1982, a man of great integrity and respected by all.

Gurney Sheppard having already practised the art of farming in Suffolk, planned the modernisation of the farms with a new corn drying and storage plant at Bluegates and a new style milking parlour and dairy to house over 200 cows in Elbrook Lane, which produces over 6,000 pints of milk every day.

It was nearly fifty years since Oswald Fordham had sold off Bear Farm when Gurney bought back the farm's land and added it once again to the Bury estate. This would have pleased old E K Fordham, who had built up the estate during the nineteenth century and died in 1889.

Now the combined farms' land is all worked from Bluegates Farm, and the crops are wheat, barley, sugar beet, oil seed rape and maize.

Farming on the outskirts

Perhaps it is just coincidence, but whereas the families running the big acreage farms were traditionally Church of England, those on the outskirts tended to be Nonconformists. Those on the western reaches were Methodists - the Harradines and the Jarmans.

These farmed land belonging to Hertfordshire County Council, broken up into smallish parcels - 30 acres or so. **Stanley Jarman**, at Ashwell End Farm, who had just over 30 acres pre-war in Ashwell and another farm in Cambridgeshire, grew vegetables for market, bred and fattened up pigs - up to 300, and kept cattle and poultry. During the Second World War, the number of pigs allowed was severely rationed - there simply was not enough foodstuffs. Stanley had more cattle, grew sugar beet and was allowed back the beet pulp to feed the cattle, supplemented by chaff mixed with bran, oats and beans. Instead of pigs, the piggeries were filled with chaff - mainly from John Sale's farm.

Roy Jarman, towards the end of the war, and younger brother Hugh after it had finished, came into the farm, acquired more land so that it stood at about 70 acres, bred more pigs through to retirement in the early nineties. Battery hens were another speciality. Much of their farm was on the land worked by the Coproliters and Roy relates how he found odd spots where small pipes of coprolite were found. (Incidentally, we need to apologise to Roy - in 'A Different World' we ascribed ownership of Walkden's clunch pits to his brother.) Various members of the **Harradine** family farmed in this area. Arther was brother to Cushi and shared the Loves Farm buildings. Arthur was known as 'Wartime' Harradine. During the First World War, as he fed his horse one morning with chaff, but without the usual ration of oats, the horse turned its head towards him and neighed. "I know", Arthur replied, "but it's wartime". His son, Douglas, decided that farming was not the life for him but, as related elsewhere, played a leading role first in the Methodist Chapel and later at the United Reformed.

Cushi Harradine lived in part of Loves Farmhouse with his family, and Albert Sheldrick recalls that when Bray's the Builders in 1950 were fixing the copper canopy over the entrance to the Methodist Chapel at Hinxworth, Cushi told him that it was in that little chapel that he had found the Lord. Sadly, like its counterpart at Ashwell, it closed down, but instead of being demolished it was transformed into a dwelling place; the copper canopy is still there.

William Holloway, who was another tenant farmer from the First World War, had as a young man scared the womenfolk at West End, when he appeared before them as a ghost, jumping off the Westbury Farm wall. As a flourishing poultry farmer, he was joined by nephew, **Roy Holloway**, in the Second World War as Roy's eyesight had prevented him from pursuing a career in the Air Force. Roy and his wife continued to run the farm, although his eyesight deteriorated into blindness, until his wife died suddenly in January 1990. Roy retired to live in Back Street. Like his uncle before him, who walked round the village daily with his friends, Jim Davies and Boer War Veteran and Poacher, Percy Dellar (collectively known as 'The Three Wise Men'), Roy walks and talks his way round much of the village, not allowing his disability to prevent his perambulations.

Above: *A dramatic photograph of straw burning.* (Lindsay Colquhoun)

Below: *A bright July evening darkened by smoke from straw burning.* (Eric Gurney)

George Longley was another Nonconformist of the Brethren persuasion, who farmed pre-war along Station Road, eventually settling down on the site of what is now known as Sunnymead Orchard. Although his poultry business failed, and the corn merchant business was never the same after Bert Gurney left in 1948 to start his own, and the Dairy Farm was only partially viable, closing down in the 1950s, the Mobile Home site his daughter Joyce started in the 1960s has been carried on with great success ever since.

George was a man of high principle and as his daughter, Joyce (now living in Edinburgh), tell us, his aim was to "make financial use of otherwise unused land, and to make homes for people in a happy atmosphere, where they knew there was someone in charge who cared about them". Opposite to Sunnymead Orchard lies the Northern's farm, and the Northern family are staunch adherents of Zoar Baptist Chapel, ie more Nonconformists.

Farmers and the environment

Although they work close to nature, and probably more than most producers take the environment seriously, economic pressures both during and after the Second World War helped to revolutionise farming practices. Scientists improved the yields by the use of fertilisers, insecticides and pesticides to an extent that was building up dangerous levels of chemical residues, such as nitrates. The growth of organic farming can be seen as a reaction. Mechanisation was also a very important factor in achieving higher yields at less cost.

Two practices became popular with farmers in the 1960s and 70s - aerial crop spraying and straw burning.

The former was a very speedy method of spraying but if inaccurately applied could cause, at the least, discomfort - sore eyes and throats, headaches etc - or even worse, actual illness. Some attributed the deaths of Sam Worboys and Raymond Christy to spraying without proper protection. Some allotment holders and gardeners discovered their crops of cabbages and other vegetables ruined by spray that strayed. The many complaints brought a change of policy. Tractors were adapted so they could carry wide spreads of spray and by the 1980s aerial spraying had virtually ended.

Coming to an enforced end in 1992 was straw burning. With the demise of the general horse population, demand for straw dropped significantly, while the increased straw yields aggravated the farmers' problem as to where to put the straw. But farmers could be careless and thoughtless towards the village population and Ruby Gurney will never forget the occasion when, in the middle of the afternoon - she had only recently come to live in the village - everything outside went dark and a terrifying noise could be heard. "Boy" Farr was burning the neighbouring field. Frequently, fields awaiting harvesting would be burnt down - a spark from a nearby field would jump the bare earth barriers.

Happily, this has now ended and somehow the excess straw will be disposed of.

The above bottles are rare examples of our drink manufacturing industry.
(The Image Studio/Cortney Publications)

Right: *Guess the year from the prices!*

A late entry: Stan Whitehead standing by Eddie Brown's van, with shop in b ackground.
(Andrew Whitehead)

In factory or workshop

1939 was to bring upheaval to the lives of many. The young were called on to fight, many of the men left behind had to change their jobs to help the war effort, and many girls and women went out of the village to help make weapons of war, or in the case of the land, make up for the loss of farm workers.

Ashwell in 1939 had a well-established reputation for manufacturing both alcoholic and non-alcoholic beverages. Fordham's Coronation Ale for the 1937 Coronation of King George VI was just one of the many beers made by the Brewery. While Page's Brewery had left mainly one legacy - the Village Hall, formerly its Maltings, and had finished about 1920, Fordham's had gone from strength to strength. From obscure beginnings in the 1820s, it now employed over 50 people, although during the war itself it suffered from an acute shortage of staff.

After the war, things got back to something like normality, but not for long.

In 1954, Flower's Brewery took over, but this time it seemed like a family reunion, because Richard Flower had married Elizabeth (born in 1764), the youngest sister of George Fordham of Sandon Bury. They named their son Edward Fordham Flower, and in due course Flowers came to Ashwell to learn the art of brewing.

Then in 1961 came the final takeover, this time by Whitbreads; huge tankers of stout came to the Mill Street brewery to be bottled and Ashwell beer was no longer made. It seemed the end was near. It came in 1965.

The premises stood empty and neglected. There were suggestions that they be converted into small units for light industry, something which Ashwell needed. But it was said that buildings so substantially built would cost too much to be converted.

So the Brewery was pulled down, except for the offices, which were made into a house. In 1973, The Maltings were converted to residential use and awarded a North Herts District Council Civic Award in 1975. Also in 1973, a bungalow and five houses were erected on a new road named Fordham Close, overlooking the stream where from time to time a kingfisher can be seen.

At the end of this Close, the brewery garage, formerly the stable block, was renovated in 1976 and the conversion, like that of the Mill House by Peter Boston, also received a North Herts District Council Commendation.

The old waterwheel, set in motion again in 1977, had been rescued from the Brewery by Peter.

In the yard behind Kirby Manor, **Frank and Percy Christy** ran their **Mineral Water Factory** and produced all sorts of soft drinks, which they supplied to the pubs and shops in Ashwell and elsewhere. Somewhat incongruously, they ran a coal supply business in the same yard, although reasonably well away from the mineral waters. The coal, transported from Ashwell Station, was bagged and distributed from the yard.

Frank Christy retired in 1953, his brother having died a few years earlier, and sold the business to Fred and John Bray and Albert Moule. By the time the Neaves Brothers took over in 1968, the mineral factory had closed down. They ran the coal business, leaving Mary Radford in charge of the shop. Bob Neaves

Fordham's Brewery c. 1920 L to R: the roof of the stables, the barrel washing shed, the loading platform, the boiler house, the stoker standing in the doorway. Extreme right the steep slated roof of one of the maltings. Demolished in 1973. (Museum)

Filling coal sacks in A&C Christy's yard behind Kirby Manor, mid-1940's. L to R: Lol Bryant, Frank Haylock, Bill Barton. (Mrs Bryant)

had been left a substantial sum by an aunt, thus enabling him to buy the two businesses. Unfortunately, they could not support his lifestyle and the businesses ended in 1973.

Byron Searle, who had taken over Bert Brown's Sunday Newspapers Agency in February 1968, in 1973 bought the Newsagency part of the Neaves' business which he and his wife, Fay, have been carrying on ever since.

The other mineral water company, R White's, occupied the Maltings in Green Lane, using them as a depot for storing their lemonade, etc. In the 1980s, they vacated the building which in the early 90s was converted into luxury flats. So in less than 50 years, a drink-making tradition of nearly 175 years had disappeared.

The building trade

1993 saw the demise of W A & F Bray Builder, whose roots were in the last century. F J Bailey & Co, after building Ashwell School in the late 1870s, became the biggest builders in and around Ashwell, employing about 50 people. These included Walter and Fred Bray, and when John Bailey retired in 1934, they took over, renaming the firm. Most of the Bailey workforce were taken on, so the changeover went smoothly, continuing to work for the same clients - the Bury Estate, the farmers, the Church authorities, Herts County Council, Hitchin Rural District Council and many others.

When the war came and most of the men were called up for military service, Walter, who was not in the best of health, retired and Fred carried on as Fred Bray, Builder. When the war ended, John came back and W A & F Bray resurfaced and was soon involved in Council house building, which Fred left to one team, while he supervised and worked on other projects.

After Bluegates' house had been added to and altered by Brays in 1949, Fred was extremely pleased when Mrs Fordham told him that she could now embark on further building work because the Public Trustee, who looked after her affairs, had informed her that she had very good value in the work done at Bluegates. A few years later, Sir Albert Richardson, the architect, presented Fred with a copy of one of his books inscribed 'To Fred Bray, the best builder I know'.

Fred Bray died in 1960 and John carried on alone, taking on the repair and maintenance work of Post Offices, Telephone Exchanges and other Government buildings over a wide area, and at the same time the work of the Odsey estate and another at Sandon. In the mid 1960s, during alterations to the Rectory and Ashwell Bury by subcontractors and without proper supervision, John was taken ill and he was given an ultimatum, 'unless the Bury alterations were completed within seven days, the firm would lose the work of two of its best clients'.

With the cooperation of most of the workforce, Albert Sheldrick saw the work was completed within the time limit.

Albert has written the following personal reminiscence of Fred Bray and the building trade:

"Fred Bray died in 1960 round about the age of 65. I am not aware of any stone monument by which to check his birth date. His work is his memorial. I believe I knew Fred better than anyone, having worked with him for nigh on 30 years, and when we both worked for builder, John Bailey, I was in lodgings with Fred for three years while we were building in seven different towns and villages.

It was in 1925 that I first met Fred Bray. I had left the Merchant Taylors' school on Maundy Thursday at the age of 14, when I had the choice of working on a farm, at Fordham's brewery, cycling to work at Letchworth in a factory or the building industry, where my father pointed out that I would be learning a trade. So knowing little about building, I was sent to Newnham Road where a good quality redbrick house, costing about £800, was being built for Miss Cator, who was a school Domestic Science teacher. (Someone has since painted the red bricks white!) Then we did quite a lot of work at Ashwell Bury, which was being remodelled under the supervision of Sir Edwyn Lutyens.

The day after August Bank holiday 1925 a gang of us were taken by lorry to build a house and farm buildings for the Herts County Council's tenant, Francis Lawton, at Holwell, near Ickleford. The first job was to erect a Nissen hut to store cement, tools and us in wet weather. Next to find lodgings, we were directed to Mrs Weedon, whose husband worked at Hartleys fruit farm nearby. Mrs Weedon agreed to provide tea at 6.30 each morning and a double bed (which Fred and I had to share) from Monday to Friday night at seven shillings each per week.

In 1926, we built 26 Council houses at Station Road, Ashwell, more at Litlington, reconditioned pubs at Stevenage and Welwyn. In 1929, we built a house at Gravenhurst, Bedfordshire, where six of us lodged with Mrs Parrish and her stepmother, Mrs Peck. The photographs of Mrs Peck's two departed husbands hung on the living room wall. The old lady laughed until she cried when Fred asked which of her two spouses she would go to when she went to heaven. But there were tears when we finally said goodbye to the two old ladies. We were the first working men lodgers they had had.

About this time, Fred split up with his Cambridge lady friend, Kit. They had been courting at weekends for years. The end came when they argued as to who was the greater man - the one who had designed King's College Chapel or a fireman. Kit voted for the fireman and lost.

We were extending the Sailor Boy at Walsworth in 1933 when Fred fell in love again, but this time with a baby, the landlord's daughter's baby, and in due course he married the mother. But having been brought up as a Nonconformist, not a drop of alcohol had ever passed his lips and he insisted that his future wife and her father vacate the pub before the marriage.

I often think of the changes I have seen in building and building workers during those years since 1925, when men worked from 7.00 am to at least 5.30 pm, even on Good Friday; they had Bank Holidays off but without pay, no pay when it rained or froze, and no annual holiday until the late 1940s. They were usually a happy lot, these bricklayers, carpenters, painters and labourers who cycled into Ashwell from Bassingbourn, Litlington, Guilden Morden, Steeple Morden, Royston, Barley and Therfield, most of them ex-service men and so, as they worked, they often sang hymns such as 'Abide with me', Boer war songs, 'Goodbye Dolly', 'I'll take you home again, Kathleen', 'Don't go down the mine Dad, there's plenty of coal on top', and their war songs, 'Blighty' and a rather naughty one, 'Where are the lads of the village tonight, in Piccadilly or Leicester Square, no not there, they have gone across the water, to - the Kaiser's daughter'.

Fred Bray was a hard man but an honest one, a first class bricklayer and, later, a good builder. W A & F Bray were invited to join the newly-formed National Builders' Federation, its aims being to promote good building, but when they were told the names of some of the members, Fred threatened to pull out. Lady Barbara Newsom put it in a nutshell when she said to Fred Bray, "You are a man who does not suffer fools gladly".

It was while we were extending and modernising a cottage at Townsend Close for Doctor Lloyd Davies' gardener, Stanley Revels, in 1952 that Fred Bray had a heavy nose bleed. He laid flat out on a pile of scaffold planks with a handkerchief and a bucket of water which I changed from time to time. Fred's nephew, John Bray, who was also in the business, wanted to fetch the doctor because the blood still flowed and after an hour he agreed and John took him home.

It was about six months before Fred did any more work and then only a few hours a day, until one day in 1953 when the firm had been asked to cobweb the church roof, ready for the visit of the new rector, Rev Jack Catterick. Eric Worboys and I raised the ladder on to one of the nave beams. I got ready with a broom to climb when Fred pushed me aside and went up a few rungs, only to turn and say, "damn it, I can't do it".

So here was a man brought up as a Nonconformist, a strict abstainer who thought, to use his own words, "Sex is a very much over-rated pastime". He had lived to work and save and was now confined to his chair and a diet of tablets to keep him alive. "If I thought they would do me in I'd take the bloody lot", he told me. One day his wife brought him a glass of sherry, but he told her to pour it down the toilet. That reminds me, it was an outside toilet; the house did not have a bathroom and all washing up and ablutions were done in the shallow 1920's sink in the kitchen.

Soon after his marriage at the Letchworth Free Church, Fred told me that he had drawn up his Will which stated that if his widow should re-marry, all his estate would go to his stepson, Richard Stafford. His coffin was to be placed on the firm's lorry, surrounded by a band playing jazz music, driven to the Cambridge crematorium by Richard and his ashes sprinkled around the mulberry tree in his garden.

Cliff Bonnett and I placed the coffin on the lorry and it was driven away, but without the jazz band. If the ashes were ever sprinkled round the mulberry bush, they were soon disturbed because the excavators moved in and several executive-type houses were built on Fred's garden, and the widow did re-marry!"

W Geeves & Son were a building firm operating from Silver Street after the war. Peter Geeves took over from his father in the 1970s, and some of the last houses he built were his own and Norman Gurney's in Ashwell Street. This very popular villager died of a brain tumour in 1982 at the age of 43 and the firm came to an end soon afterwards. **I.D. Products** in Back Street, which was started in 1962 by Donald Willatts, has strong connections with the building trade as it manufactures all kinds of timber products, employing 12 people.

Lorries, coaches and taxis (AS)

The invention of the internal combustion engine, which Frank Brown told Norman Gurney had ruined farming, brought opportunities to entrepreneurs like **Albert Moule**. In the 1920s Albert drove W F Rands Builders' lorry, until he decided to become his own boss and bought a second-hand car to do evening and weekend taxi work. This was followed by a lorry and then another.

In the 1930s, after builder John Bailey had retired, Albert Moule acquired the Red House and Builders' Yard with its extensive premises in Silver Street. The haulage business was very competitive, much of it being work which involved collecting loads of potatoes, cabbages and brussels sprouts from the local farms and delivering them in the early hours to Covent Garden and Spitalfields markets. During the winter there was the locally grown sugar beet crop to be loaded and delivered to the beet processing factories at Ely, Peterborough and Bury St Edmunds.

By 1939, there was a fleet of about a dozen lorries involved in the building of airfields and other war work. For a time after the war the firm was busy clearing hidden ammunition dumps from the Bedfordshire woods.

With the extensive post-war building programme, bricks, sand and ballast were in great demand, and the lorries were working full time.

In July 1945, Joe West, just released from the West Ham Fire Brigade, where he had served as a leading fireman throughout the war, joined Albert's team of lorry drivers.

The firm went into the coach business as Blue Cream Coaches, with seaside and other outings, and a school bus contract. Juniors were brought from Newnham, Radwell and Hinxworth to the Ashwell school and seniors from all the villages taken to schools at Royston and Baldock.

With nationalisation of the haulage business, the lorries were transferred to British Road Services depot at Henlow, where Joe now worked on the office staff, until de-nationalisation in 1954. From then on, Albert took life easy, visiting his favourite hostelries, joining a golf club, and on early winter evenings enjoying driving slowly round the lanes, a gun at his side, always hoping for a shot at a stray or roosting pheasant, leaving Joe to run the business. One of Albert's longstanding contracts was for the clearance of fly ash from the Little Barford power station, some of which was sold to the builders of the M1 motorway.

The haulage business came to an end in 1969, and finally in 1976 the fleet of seven Blue Cream coaches ceased to operate, as did Albert when he reached the age of 90 in 1991.

The lorry and coach drivers were Ted Ball, Fred Brown, Will Brown, Alf Chapman, John Collins, Bill Davis, Jim Davis, Tony Eley, Pete Hankin, Percy Pettingell, Sid Sheldrick, Arthur Waldock, Sid Waldock, Brian Worboys and Theo Worboys. (I apologise if I have left out any driver.) Mechanic, Michael Cranwell, kept all the vehicles on the road. When both of the businesses came to an end, Michael set up his own as **M F Cranwell & Son**, in the same premises, appropriately as Motor Engineers and is still going strong in 1993.

Another road haulier was **Geoffrey Hall**, who operated between 1948 and 1960. Much of his work was doing the London Food Markets' run and taking beet to the beet factories.

Geoffrey was a great drinker of Guinness, acquiring an overgrown stomach, and smoked cigarettes one after the other. Because of resulting health problems, the doctors told him to cut out a lot of the food he was having, and eat chicken. Geoff assumed he meant whole chickens, which he demolished with gusto. He died in the early eighties.

Another member of Albert Moule's generation who went into the transport business was **Frank Gentle**.

In the 1920s, he was a lorry driver for Bailey's, the builders. Wanting to have his own business, he bought a lorry, and took on contract work for farmers and other customers. In 1950, he went into the coach business in Silver Street, and after expansion occupied the buildings vacated by Cliff Levings next to the Springs in 1957. Having completed his National Service, his son, Gordon, joined him and acquired the bungalow and premises on the Hinxworth Road, known as El Rancho. After his father died, Gordon carried on the business until his premature death on holiday in Portugal in 1991.

In 1950, **Fred Gallop** started a garage and coach business on a site stretching from Swan Street to the Churchyard, between the old Six Bells Pub and Burr's Row. He erected a part timber garage, did repairs and servicing, much to the annoyance of his neighbours.

His application for the installation of petrol pumps caused such friction between the Parish Council and the Rural District Council that at the former's meeting in September 1952 it was announced that in spite of the great risk of fire

Above: *Westcliff House built for Fred Bailey in the early 1900's. On the left are piles of left over building materials much of which was used to build the bungalows in Bygrave Road. In the background can be seen the scaffold poles erected for building the bungalow in which Norman Gurney's parents and family lived from 1934.* (Mrs. L. MacBeth)

Below: *The staff (over 50) of Irvin's the parachute makers, who occupied the above building from 1961-1974.* (Dorothy Cox)

to the neighbouring cottages, the nearness to the church and the strong protests of the Parish Council and individuals, the RDC had consented to the pumps for five years. In any case, the RDC claimed, the cottages would eventually be demolished. In 1993, they are still there, in excellent order, the petrol pumps have gone, but were allowed to stay for 38 years! Although the Parish Council took matters further and enlisted the help of MP, Nigel Fisher, the petrol pumps won at the expense of the parish politicians! In 1961, Fred Gallop moved to Baldock, taking his 'latest air conditioned' coaches with him. But the garage remained until 1989, happily to make way for Glenys Travis's new house, one of Bray's last and protracted constructions.

When Fred Bailey retired, he built an interesting house with a balcony known as Westcliff House) at the top of Bear Lane. When **Harry Leverett** bought it, however, he built a single storey structure, attached to the house and extending to the end of the garden. This was to be used partly as garages for buses. He installed a bus turntable and built a bus himself, which he called 'Ye Olde Tin Can'. He started Ashwell's first bus service which was then taken over by the Eastern National Bus Company. Single decker buses were garaged there, in readiness for early morning runs to get the workers to factories in Baldock, etc. Negotiating the blind corner at the top of Bear Lane was always hazardous, and Norman Gurney witnessed a nasty accident when a motor cyclist crashed into the radiator of the bus as it was halfway across the corner turn. He was badly injured.

During the war, vast quantities of newsprint in huge rolls were stored in the garages. In 1961, moving from Royston, the **Irvin Parachute Company**, employing over 50 people, mostly Ashwellians, occupied the factory. Ian Wright, then a Director of the company told Norman Gurney that the Ashwell Factory, which made parachutes for the United States Forces in Vietnam and for which it had to satisfy stringent licensing requirements, was the most efficient of all the Irvin Units. In 1948, **Bert Gurney** had a serious heart attack and when he returned to work at Longley's, his inability to do the full job of managing the corn merchanting side meant a serious loss in pay. So he started his own Corn Merchant's business in 1949, erecting buildings on the land adjacent to his home in Ashwell Street and this was very successful for, what was initially, a one-man band. Son, Eric, who was in the RAF during the 50s, helped him and when he died in 1958, Eric, with his sister Rachel and Mother, carried on the business until it was sold to Sheriffs of Hatfield in 1964. A builder's merchant leased the property until 1973. Over the next three years, four houses were built on the now vacant land for the families of Rod Leete, Norman Gurney, Peter Geeves and finally, Neville Cromey-Hawke.

In the meantime, the old Irvin Factory had been occupied by **Redbourn Plastics Ltd**. A serious fire broke out in 1974, and this may have hastened the end of this company. In the late 70s, **Cooke Engineering Ltd** bought and renovated the building and have been manufacturing nuts and bolts ever since.

We have not mentioned every single enterprise in Ashwell during our period, but we have presented a picture of much activity, of some successes and a few failures. But with the loss of the Brewery, the ever decreasing demand for farm workers, there was much concern to find rural industries to bring employment and prosperity. The result of this concern involves a later period.

Ashwell at Home

Homes for heroes (NJG)

Just before the Second World War, Mrs Fordham was reporting to Ashwell Parish Council that the Hitchin Rural District Council was planning 2 bungalows and 6 cottages for farm workers along Back Street. But war came, and they were never built. As victory over Nazi Germany began to look inevitable, in spite of doodle bugs and V2 rockets, thoughts turned to the need for new homes. As was not unusual in those days, there was conflict between the Parish Council and the Hitchin Rural District Council (RDC): where should the new homes be sited? A Labour Government with a substantial majority signalled sweeping changes at local levels. The Annual Parish Meeting at Ashwell habitually re-elected serving Councillors and when their names were called the parishioners dutifully put up their hands.

When Mrs Fordham's name was called, she usually looked over her shoulder and, as the hands shot up, she smiled and wiped her long tongue round her lips.

All that was to change in 1946, when there were 20 candidates, so for the first time ever it was necessary to hold a secret ballot and as there were several candidates for the two seats on the Hitchin Rural District Council, there was also a ballot for that.

There was some new blood on the new council and the two successful candidates for the Rural District Council, each with a large number of votes, were William E Reeves of Pleasant Place, an Ashwell businessman and Charles Walker, a civil servant in the Department of Customs and Excise, who lived at Wellesbourne, which he had built in the early 1930s.

Mrs Phyllis Fordham, who had represented Ashwell for many years, had been defeated. When, later, some people disagreed with the new men, Mrs Fordham said, "If you put them in, you must get them out".

At the Annual Parish Meeting in 1946 there was a record attendance of 180 persons, probably because it was known that housing was on the agenda. Correspondence with the RDC proved that of all the sites discussed the Bear Lane site was still the best. The meeting passed a resolution urging that the original scheme for the building of houses in Ashwell be proceeded with the utmost despatch. This was proposed by Bert Gurney.

At the meeting on 22 January 1947, it was reported that there were 70 applications for Council houses and that work would soon begin.

Six bungalows were built on part of Bear Lane meadow, Back Street, and were followed by 18 Airey-type pre-fabricated houses on the new road and later named Dixies Close.

In May 1952, the Parish Council met the Hitchin Rural District Surveyor, Mr R J Walker, and told him of their suggestions for building houses along the 'Tops'

An aerial view of Ashwell in 1947. (Aerofilms Ltd)

This picture taken from the church tower in the late 1950's – *the top third shows the council house estates of Ashwell Street and Dixies Close, the Back Street bungalows and Bear Lane houses are very clear. A little to the left is the Primary School and Schoolhouse behind. In the foreground, left hand corner, behind the Parish Room is the old*

A splendid aerial view of Ashwell in 1964. In left hand corner, note the flats and bungalows in Ashwell Street, and the additional houses in Dixies Close. A picture well worth careful study. (Aerofilms Ltd)

(ie Ashwell Street). Eventually these were built. The flats and bungalows extending to the Foresters' Allotments were not built until 1964.

The next major development was proposed in 1967 - 24 houses on the old Brewery site and on land surrounding it. Author, poet, scholar and Parish Councillor, David Holbrook, mobilised opinion against a development many considered would alter the character of the village. In the end, the Maltings were tastefully converted into two residences, Fordham Close was created with a bungalow and 5 houses, and at the end the old stables, now a lorry garage, transformed into the Dray House.

In 1968, another major development was proposed - 18 houses on a site named Woodforde Close, after Dr Woodforde, Ashwell's doctor for 33 years. Although the Parish Council had many misgivings and secured quite a few changes to the original plan, the 18 houses were built early in the 1970s.

A welcome provision was the building of Wolverley House, providing self-contained flats for Ashwell's senior citizens, erected on Mrs Fordham's kitchen garden off Gardiners Lane. This was a great achievement and in the late 70s the village raised enough money for a lift to be installed.

Pressure for more housing was being applied from the numbers wanting to come and live in Ashwell: it was seen as a desirable village to commute to work and back. Professionals and middle executives were being attracted, and these were the type of people who mostly bought up the homes in Woodforde Close.

News of an even bigger development then broke - the Angell farming family had had a tempting offer to sell their Silver Street meadow for £250,000 and between 1975 and 1978 44 houses were built on the site, logically named Angells Meadow. Other developments were completed before 1976 - The Rickyard in Back Street, a small courtyard of 8 houses built in the place of Dixies Farm Cart Hovel.

Between 1976 and 1978 the old Bluegates Dairy in the High Street, with its thatched milking parlour and other buildings, came down and were replaced by Bacon's Yard - an estate of 14 houses and flats. Dixies Farmyard, with its old boarded barns, was sold to developers. Some barns were split into units for small businesses and others, in the early 80s, converted into houses with pocket handkerchief-sized gardens.

In that influential document, Ashwell Village Appraisal 1976, it was pointed out that between 1970 and 1978 new houses built or definitely planned would mean a growth of nearly 25% of its housing stock. Broadly speaking, this is what happened.

Part of the impetus for the establishment of the Ashwell Association was the way in which a major development could be 'sprung' upon the village with little real opportunity to challenge or change it if need be, and without it fitting into a planned development recognised by planners and parishioners alike.

The publication of the County Structure Plan was a recognition by the planners that longer term planning rather than piecemeal development was a much better framework in which all concerned could work, and the Appraisal Document was a landmark for Ashwell. The subjects it dealt with included Agricultural Land and Buildings, Employment, Health and Welfare, Education and Community Activities.

Above: *The Engine, Back Street, in 1975, named after the Steam Engine. Was a pub in 1836, taken over by Fordhams in 1873. Albert Covington was the popular landlord in the 1950's . Closed in 1993.* (Philip Coverdale/Museum)

Below: *The great fire of 1850 ended in Jessamine House. Although built in the 16th century, it has a Georgian front. During World War II became the offices of the London tea merchants Ferguson Holness. Until recently it housed the offices of the Veteran Car Club of Great Britian. 1978.* (Philip Coverdale/Museum)

Above: *Alms Lane. On the right the first Telephone Exchange, now demolished. The Parish Room with dormer windows before the 1970's renovation.* (Hertfordshire Countryside)

Above right: *Cob Walls. The thatched cob wall in Gardiners Lane was repaired and re-thatched in 1973. Ashwell was noted for its cob walls. In the late 1800's an old Ashwellian listed those that remained then. Apart from the iron fence in front of Dixies farm house, the rest of the meadow was surrounded by a cob wall until the 1920's. Another divided No 86 High Street from Bacon's Yard, until it was destroyed in 1978 by the builders. This one originally linked up with the Gardiners Lane wall which entirely enclosed the Bury kitchen gardens, where Wolverley House has since been built. The Forresters cottages had a cob wall in Hodwell, and the remains of another one can still be seen along the footpath to the Springs. And still another cob wall was to be seen at the top of Angell's Meadow until the 1930's.* (Gurney Sheppard)

Dove Cottages (1975) overlooking the Springs. Note remains of Cob Wall.

(Philip Coverdale/Museum)

Many of its key recommendations have been fulfilled.

For example, its view that any development of large areas as estates should be banned; development on the fringes of the village should stop; any development on Dixies Meadow should be vigorously opposed; tree stocks should be replenished and hedgerows preserved. The maintenance of existing shops should be encouraged; agricultural land and buildings must be preserved and adapted to new purposes where necessary; the Further Education Centre must not be allowed to close; the Village Hall structure and facilities should be improved; a street cleaner should be employed.

Not all of its recommendations have been carried out. We do not have a supplementary private bus service, although the taxi services to and from the Station are much better organised now; the provision of low cost rented accommodation has not been achieved, in spite of the excellent work of the Ashwell Housing Association and its major success - the development in Bear Farm, referred to below.

Hypermarkets should be avoided! Three have been established in Baldock, Letchworth and Royston.

The Appraisal foresaw the need for additional surgery and other health provisions which have largely been achieved with the building of the new Surgery, opened in May 1989.

So the authors of the Appraisal can be well satisfied.

Since 1978, the role of the Ashwell Association has gradually diminished - mainly because its main objectives have been accomplished and the Parish Council now gives detailed scrutiny to planning applications. Its standard bearers - Sue Morris, Jim Graham, and Ann Reddaway are owed much by the village.

The Ashwell Housing Association was born out of a Working Party set up in 1972 by the Ashwell Association and in 1979 the first lettings occurred of the property built or adapted on short Bear Lane and Bear Farm Site in Back Street - 2 bungalows, 4 3-bedroom houses and 4 flats.

The Housing Association's protracted efforts to purchase the old Dairy Site in High Street were eventually thwarted. It carries on, but for any small Housing Association the problems, legal and logistic, are very daunting.

How the foresters' cottages were saved (AS)

The oak timbers and whitewashed walls of the Foresters' cottages in High Street, Ashwell, are quite a feature. Ask how old they are and you will be given a range of dates from the 14th to the 16th century.

My first memories, in the twenties, are of five whitewashed cottages with very little timber showing. They were occupied at No 1 by a brewery worker, Julius Covington, his wife and the son of Mrs Covington's unmarried sister. At No 2 by Arthur Covington (not related), whose daughter married Alf Ketteridge, the garage owner. George (known as Swannee) Worboys, with his wife and bachelor sons, George and Ned, lived at No 3 and at No 4 Bill Revel resided with his sister Annie. Bill was a farm worker and on Sundays pumped the church organ; Annie worked in the bottling department of Fordham's brewery. A rather doddery old man lived at No 5, who at one time kept ponies and traps in the tythe barn in Church Lane, destroyed by fire early this century.

Not wishing to lower the tone of this chapter, I will merely say that his daughter had more men visitors than she had hot dinners.

The above-mentioned tenants were members of the Ancient Order of Foresters. Towards the end of the 1950s the committee of the AOF took stock of their assets. Fewer young men were joining, older members were passing on so Bray's the builders were asked to tidy up the property with a view to selling it. (Walter, Fred and John Bray were all members of the AOF.) Fred Bray, Cliff Bonnett and I replaced missing roof tiles, repaired outside plasterwork and whitewashed the walls. We discovered that one roof timber over George Worboys' bedroom had dropped. Rather than disturb the frail old man, Fred decided that the timber was in no way dangerous and could be replaced when the cottage was vacant, at a cost of about £14.

During 1959 the club officials, with the consent of the AOF head office, put up the cottages for sale by auction at the Three Tuns.

The purchaser was a Mr J Ibbotson, a businessman; as far as I remember, the price was £2,500. Rumour said that he had been offered £7,000 for the site minus the cottages. 'A nice little earner', as TV's Arthur Daley would have said. Some Ashwell people will remember that a year or so earlier the old Bull's Head pub had been bought by Mr Ibbotson. Apart from that section of the pub now known as Beams, the rest was built with Stotfold stock bricks under a good slate roof and was occupied by two families. The man who removed some slates from the roof ready for the Council's surveyor to inspect, told me that the roof was in very good condition. However, the official condemned the property, and most of it was pulled down. At a later date the part now known as Beams was reconditioned and put up for sale and the remaining land stretching from High Street back to Silver Street was sold. Plans for a block of flats were turned down, but eventually a pair of well-designed houses were built alongside Beams and a similar pair in Silver Street.

In November 1959, Mr R J Walker, Surveyor to the Hitchin Rural District Council, accompanied by the HRD Sanitary Inspector (he now has a much grander name), inspected the five Foresters' cottages. The latter was then sent to inform the tenants (only three of the cottages were occupied at that time) that the whole block of property was unsafe and gave them 24 hours' notice to get out. The tenants refused and were taken to Royston magistrates' court on several occasions. At first the magistrates pointed out that if the property was so dangerous a notice should have been fixed to each door stating that fact, also a hoarding should have been placed to protect passers-by. Eventually their Worships weakened and granted eviction orders in January 1960.

Very early on the following Monday morning a demolition gang were at work smashing the old roof tiles, while plumbers were removing water pipes and cutting off the supply, and the Electricity Board not only removed the meters but dug up the pavement to remove the cables.

Very soon the telephone wires were humming between Ashwell and the Hertfordshire Society and the Society for The Preservation of Ancient Buildings. These two bodies acted swiftly. Their architects examined the buildings and stated that the damaged timber could be quite easily and cheaply renewed, confirming Fred Bray's earlier report.

The two bodies made their report to the then Minister of Housing and Local Government and at midday on Thursday a special courier arrived at the site with a temporary preservation order and demanded that demolition cease.

The following Tuesday, 2 February 1960, the Rural District Council met as usual at Hitchin, questions were asked about the cottages, the Clerk said that his office had been flooded with letters and telephone calls about the property. Mr Walker, the Surveyor, said they were not necessarily going to pull the property down, just stripping the roof and back walls to see how far the rot had gone; in their present state they were even more dangerous than before. (No one asked him why the plumbing and electricity cables had been taken or why the roof tiles were smashed instead of being stored for re-use.) The Council then decided that the matter should not be discussed in public and the Clerk added, "There's a whole lot of legal problems involved here". A few days later I saw a television crew filming the wrecked building; I stopped to speak to the man in charge, Bob Wellins, who at that time was with Anglia Television, and asked him to tell the whole truth about the Foresters' cottages. He replied, "We have only been here ten minutes and we find the whole thing stinks". The ancient skeleton stood for months and refused to fall down, proving that the Surveyor had made a mistake. Eventually it was bought by Hertfordshire County Council by compulsory purchase, divided into three houses and restored to something like its original condition.

An excellent photograph of the timber frame appeared in the Guardian of 7 July 1962 with this caption, 'A fourteenth century building at Ashwell Herts stripped to its timber frame in the process of restoration. Foresters' Cottages were saved from demolition by local action and are now being rebuilt as dwellings by the County Council. The work is being supervised by Sir Albert Richardson'.

At about this time I took a party of Hitchin visitors round the village and told them the story of the cottages so far. Several of the people remarked, "Hitchin has lost some of its old buildings in the last few years. If a village such as Ashwell can do it, so can we". Shortly afterwards I heard that a Hitchin Society had been formed.

Pargetry (AS)

Early in 1948, I was sent to examine the plasterwork on the front of the block of property in High Street which includes Days the Bakers. Early this century the whole frontage of the cottages and the shop had been plastered in the form of panels, with each panel having a six-inch band surrounding it. The old lime, sand and hair plaster was perished and had been falling onto the pavement for years. Both Mrs Janet Beresford, who owned the cottages and Days, the shop, had decided to have the plasterwork repaired or patched. I found that it was beyond repair, but behind the plaster I saw sound oak timbers, some of which I exposed.

The buildings had not been scheduled as of historic interest, simply because Hitchin Rural District Council officials had decided in 1937 to demolish them. So it was merely for the two owners of the property to determine whether to strip

After nearly a century in Mill Street as a horse mounting block, a bollard and an anti-invasion obstacle, the Dixies Stone was brought back to its home at Dixies Farm on Nov 13th 1948.
L to R: Bert Brown, Maurice Brown, Richard Stafford, Albert Sheldrick, Albert Brown, Fred Bray and seated on the stone, Eric Gurney and Michael Revel. (A. W. Sheldrick)

The Foresters' Cottages were rescued from complete demolition in 1959. (Mrs E. C. Brown)

The Recreation Ground: *Newly planted trees, concrete posts and rail have replaced the fine elm trees killed by disease. The 1960 pavilion to the left, the old pavilion to the right, children's play area between. 1970's.* (Museum)

Kingsland Way formerly known as Lime Kiln Lane c. 1925. Steps on both sides lead up to the cottage front doors. The baker's cart with a dog underneath suggests that this is Days' who were always dog lovers. (David Harris)

and replaster or strip and expose the timber frame as it was when the property was built some four or five hundred years earlier. Fortunately, they decided on the latter option.

So Fred Bray, Cliff Bonnett and I carefully removed the three copper Atlas insurance plaques, stripped off the plaster and laths, then, after treating the timbers with a wood preservative, replastered between the oak timbers, whitewashed the panels and replaced the insurance signs. At the same time we carefully repaired the damaged plaster pargetry on the cottage next door which is wrongly named the Guild house.

On 29 September 1948, the local newspaper, The Hertfordshire Pictorial (now The Comet), announced 'Now Ashwell (where the Duke of Clarence drowned in claret) is wearing a proud new look'. The caption with their photograph of the Restored Guild Hall of St John the Baptist states, 'The old and the new. Ashwell's old cottages have been renovated - and in the background a television aerial rises above the roof tops'.

The Duke of Clarence (one of the patrons of the Guild) is said to have been drowned in a butt of malmsey wine, but not at Ashwell.

Above: R to L: *Part of the Guildhouse. The cottage next door after the pargetting had been restored. Bert Collis' Cycle Shop.*

Right: *A common sight pre-1939 – The Privy otherwise known as the Necessary or Dunnikin down under! Inside was a boxed in seat with a hole in the centre and bucket underneath. When it was nearly full, the contents were dug into the vegetable garden – said to be extremely good for rhubarb. Lindsay Colquhoun who bought this particular model from the Bray sale, is going to erect it in his garden for ornamental and historic purposes.*

A Village of Shopkeepers (NJG)

At the opening of our period 1939 to 1975, Ashwell was well served with its 20 shops. By 1975, there was still a thriving retail trade, but choice and numbers had been considerably reduced and these shops, small by supermarket standards, could not compete on equal terms. If we travel through the village east to west and then back again, the first activity we came across in 1939 would have been shoe repairing in the hut-like shop of Tommy Knott, who lived in the adjoining cottage next to the Springs. In 1953, having moved from his workshop in Silver Street, **Cliff Levings** had Tommy's shop for car and tractor repairs. Cliff was a most talented man, able to turn his hand to almost anything mechanical, and could repair clocks, televisions, radios, as well as cars. At the age of eight, he was helping with the harvesting when the binder broke down - the complex mechanisms making the string tie up each sheaf went wrong. The men working it tried all they knew, and failed, but Cliff told them what needed to be done and, with a few deft manipulations, put the mechanism right. In later years, Cliff drank too much for his own good, his business ended in the mid 50's and he went to work at George Turner's Garage, further along the High Street. In spite of being almost blind, he could see and feel enough or hear enough to be able to repair the faults in a car better than most.

Frank Gentle ran his coach business here after Cliff left.

Eventually the coach business moved to El Rancho along the Hinxworth Road, run by Gordon and Marjorie Gentle until the former's untimely death in 1991.

Just past the Three Tuns was the **wheelwright's workshop** - an ancient barn - of saintly Silas Worboys, Methodist local preacher and a great character. His partner was Wilfred Bryant. If you had a few minutes to spare, you could watch him at his work, making the cartwheels and other farm implements. He died in 1953 and his barn was demolished right at the end of our period.

As we go further west, we walk past the Foresters' Cottages and Vine Cottage, formerly the Dun Cow Pub, we would have come in 1939 to **Westrope's**, in existence then for approximately 80 years. Trading as C H Westrope, the spacious premises included Grocery, Provisions and Wines. The 'Store for Quality and Service' had departments in Drapery, Outfitting, Boots and Shoes, Hardware, China, Glass and Garden Supplies. This mini emporium had competitors in J H Christy and Son, now known as Ashwell Stores, and a few other smaller shops in the village. But even if Gin was more than the 2/- a bottle it was in the 1880s, all the shops charged the same prices for brand items; wherever you bought Tate and Lyle's sugar, Golden Meadow or Golden Acre Butter, Lyons or Mazawatti Tea, you would pay the same. On the other hand, Westrope's had its own blend - 'Ashwell Tea'.

This all changed in 1973, when the Heath government abolished Resale Price Maintenance and shops could charge what they liked, to a large extent.

During the Second World War, food was rationed but most had enough to eat. Indeed it has been said that the nation was never healthier. There were not many of the ugly overhanging stomachs which we see today.

Above: *Pre-1939, but cannot be left out: On the right hand side next to the Springs the shop and house where Tommy Knott and later Cliff Levings and Frank Gentle had businesses for a time.* (Mrs. L. MacBeth)

Above right: *Terry Crump the fishmonger on his round, 1960's.* (Marjorie Gentle)

Above: *C. H. Westrope's delivery van c.1920.* (P. Crump)
Right: *A rare sight even in the 1960's – the Scissor Grinder near Dixies farm.* (Mrs. E. C. Brown)

T.D. Dennis. the family butcher, and pre-Christmas display of turkeys. c. 1960. (Mrs E. C. Brown)

M. V. Crump's the Family Butchers celebrate the Queen's Jubilee in 1977 . L to R: *John Simmons, Jonathan Crump, Richard Crump, Robert Chandler, Geraldine Crump, Peter Bryant, Joyce Collins, Philip Crump, Nancy Eversden, Terry Crump, David Crump.* (Philip Crump)

Eddie Brown's butcher's shop in the house next door to the chemists below. (Doris Shelton)

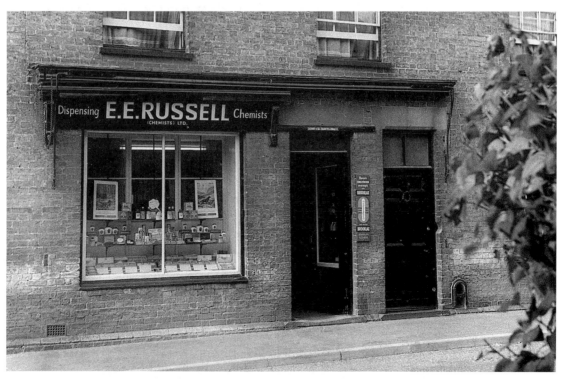

E. E. Russell dispensing chemists. 1953. *A chemist's shop since the mid-1800's in the High Street now Country Properties.* (Terry Knight)

By the year of the coronation of Queen Elizabeth II, 1953, butter, cheese, milk, meat and bacon were still rationed, although it was possible once again to buy coffee or the bottled Camp coffee and chicory, with a picture of the general who, in World War I had said, "Your Country needs you". Britain was still a nation of tea drinkers - leaf tea of course - Lyons, and Mazawatti tea, in 1/4lb, 1/2lb or 1lb packets at 5s 4d per pound. Cadbury's were making a drinking chocolate at 1s 5d per 1/2lb, McVities' Digestive biscuits were 1s 0d per 1/2lb, and Hartley's Raspberry Jam 1s 6d per 1lb jar. A 12oz tin of corned beef cost 3/- and a tin of Heinz chicken soup 1s 1d. Shippams Meat or Fish paste was 10d a pot. To the few people who had a 'fridge', a 1/2lb of Birds Eye Frozen Peas cost 1s 7d. For the sweet-toothed, Maltesers were 1s 6d a box, Spangles, advertised as the 'Fruitiest sweet ever', were 2d per packet and Bounty, the new chocolate and coconut bar, was just being introduced.

For washdays, Persil was taking the place of the old faithfuls, Rinso and Oxydol. Many people still used Lifebuoy or Wright's Coal Tar soap, but if the adverts were to be believed, half of Britain preferred the pleasant smell of Palmolive, while some 'just loved Lux' soap flakes, because nine out of ten film stars used Lux.

The smoker who before the war and during the war had paid sixpence for ten, or a shilling for twenty of the best cigarettes, now paid 3s 9d for twenty of the best and 3s 7d for the other brands. A few years previously Charles Westrope died suddenly in January 1948. There were various changes of management and later ownership. For a few years the Harrison and Waldock families ran the business very efficiently but by the late sixties, village shopkeepers were being whittled away by the supermarkets. Ron Blake and his wife took over in the seventies, but their efforts to keep the business going ended in the early eighties when they told their customers by letter that the shop was closing due to lack of support. On a happier note, after the premises had been drastically redeveloped, two small shops opened - **Ashwell Chemists**, with an Indian lady pharmacist, Mrs Raksha McCann, and a **Greengrocery** business belonging to Mr and Mrs Thompson of Shingay, much to everyone's delight, and are still going strong in 1993, seven years later.

Ashwell Chemists have a long tradition for their enterprise as well as their pharmaceutical abilities, and early this century W H Bridgman occupied the premises a few doors from Westropes, now rented by the **Estate Agents, Country Properties**. Ashwell chemists not only sold remedies, they made them. Mr Bridgman claimed his Blood Purifier Tonic could cure nearly everything! E E Russell, the Letchworth Chemists, bought the shop in the 1930s and it remained in their possession until Kingswoods added it to their chain of chemist shops around 1973. Ashwell's pharmacist at that time was Scotsman Adam Barr, who retired in 1985 at the age of 73. The shop and surrounding premises, part of which he and his wife Cynthia occupied, had been sold about that time to a property developer, John Bush, in which Grant Boughton who opened an Estate Agency replacing the Chemist's Shop, played a part. For a few months, Ashwell was for the first time for over a century without a chemist.

Eddie Brown, a Methodist local preacher, took over Jack Ashwell's Butcher's Shop, situated in Ventnor House, in the late 40s; behind it he had a Slaughter

House and advertised "Home Killed Meat of Best Quality". Its hygienic arrangements were not, however, of the highest quality and on one occasion in Jack Ashwell's time a Health Inspector threw creosote over a slaughtered cow which was diseased, to prevent its sale to unsuspecting customers! Eddie was well known for his ability to smoke the full length of a cigarette to its stub without dropping the ash - or taking it out of his mouth or stop talking, but behind the counter, on the floor was a continuous line of ash and cigarette stubs! Hardly up to European Community standards of hygiene. To nearly every remark made to him he replied 'Too true!', which became his nickname. Stan Whitehead carried on for a time after Eddie retired in the early 1960s and the shop closed down in the late sixties. Stan was an inveterate smoker and, like Eddie, died of lung cancer. In later life, Eddie, widowed some years earlier, after retirement had married Ivy Harvey, well known as one of the finest sopranos in Hertfordshire and organist at the United Reformed Church until 1992.

Just before the second World War, you would have witnessed the rather sad end of Fanny Adkin's shop, on the west corner of Church Lane. During the War, the house was partly occupied by evacuees, a watchmaker and others.

Eventually it became the **Surgery**, which moved in 1953 from the old Saddlery premises, now occupied by **Ian Walters'** photographic business, and remained there until the purpose built surgery opened in 1990.

Next door, almost bang in the centre of the village, was **Turner's Garage**, originally started by Alf Ketteridge in the 1920s, later taken over by a Hitchin firm, and managed during and after the War by George Turner, who eventually formed a partnership with John Bailey and Charles Westrope to buy it in the 40s. When he retired in the late 1960s, Fred Turner, no relationship to George, and his wife ran it.

Whilst highly conscientious, a good engineer, assisted by a skilled and helpful staff, he was unable to resist taking on extra work even if this meant owners with cars already in the garage for repair could be kept waiting, sometimes for weeks.

Making continuous and desperate efforts to reduce his backlog, Fred's garage would be open from early morning to 10 or 11 o'clock at night, much to the annoyance of the immediate neighbourhood.

You could shop pre-war at the **Co-op** in Ashwell in the property now known as Stag House, formerly the Stag Public House, and managed by Stan and Rene Raven, from 1939 to 1954. Part of the Letchworth, Hitchin and District Cooperative Society, it advertised Grocery, Butchery, a Mutuality Club, and deliveries of Bread, Confectionery, Milk, Coal and other Fuels. At the back of the shop, wheat, bran and other supplies for the numerous households who kept chickens and other livestock in their back gardens.

Stan Raven, known as 'Skip', was a keen Scouting man, and when the evacuees came in 1939 he formed the boys into a Scout troop, later amalgamating with the Ashwell Troop. Stan and Rene have now retired to Kings Lynn.

The Co-op in Ashwell closed down in the early 1960s.

The building attached to Stag House, and adjoining Alms Lane, is a very old one (16th century) and through its chequered history it has frequently been involved with trade of some description. It was the home of carpenter, Herbert Picking, and later used for radio repairs. During the war, Florrie Brown, whose

71

husband was an officer billeted in The Maltings, was sent by a Hitchin salon to attend to the hair of Ashwell ladies once a week, and around the end of the war Alice Anderson bought and renovated the premises and from then on it was a Hairdressing Salon. **Sue Birch** took it over towards the end of our period - August 1974 to be precise, and in 1993 she is still carrying on the noble tonsorial art.

The High Street at one time had at least nine public houses (between Bear Lane and the Springs), one of which was the Two Brewers. Now long gone, it was bought in 1937 by **William Searle**, father to Byron, and run as a Confectioners and Tobacconists. Vegetables and Fruit were also supplied and the shop became known as **'Bottom Searle's'**. You could enjoy afternoon tea served by Doris Thompson, later married to Bob Davies - tragically she died from cancer at an early age leaving behind two small children. A Saloon Car was available for hire, belonging to the enterprising William. Fonce Waldock took over in 1946 and sold it to Mrs Curtis in 1950, who kept the shop going for another 10 years or so.

We now come to the dangerous junction of High Street and Gardiners Lane and a visiting stranger would have looked with amazement at the skilled work of a topiarist, the top of the shop fascia being garlanded with evergreen shrubs, trained into beautiful shapes. A centrepiece was a carved Bull's Head, so this was Tommy Dennis's Butcher's shop which he had acquired in 1931, although he rented the premises soon after World War I. Tommy was a great character and showman and his conjuring tricks at Village Hall Shows were very popular; as he got older, he disliked going grey - he was always very smart with well groomed wavy hair and he used to put butter on it to keep it black! Unfortunately, as he got warmer and warmer in the shows, it started to melt and run down his face! In 1965, Mr Kingsley took over and 12 years later a Mr Hughes followed but not for long, as he went bust. Two years passed before the shop was occupied and this time there was a complete change of use : Graham and Sheila Swallow opened it as a Confectioners, Stationers Greetings Cards plus Household Electrical Supplies. When the Cherry's took on the premises in the 1980s, you could order your coal as well, as Mr Cherry ran a Coal Merchant's business from Steeple Morden where they lived.

The shop next door had been trading for about 150 years, some have claimed from 1540. In the 1948 Show Programme, J H Christy and Son Ltd advertised as **'Ashwell's Universal Stores'**. From their advertisement you can see they had a wide range of goods and were also ironmongers. In the 1940s, Hannah Day, Joan and Jeff Wilson were involved in the running of the shop. In 1951 Goosey Sackett took it over and ran it till 1963. Then Eric and Audrey Gurney were in charge until 1965. They energetically trebled Goosey's weekly turnover from £200 to £600, helped by the closure of the Co-op, a hundred yards away. The pressures of bringing up a young family when you're open all hours and Eric's farming ambitions beginning to materialise, the shop was sold to Mr & Mrs Thomas. In the 1970 Show Programme, the phrase 'Your VG Food Store' appears and the shop is called **'Ashwell Stores'**.

About this time, small grocers were getting together to buy through one major supplier to get the best possible prices. It is also apparent by the end of our period that non-food items had largely disappeared. After various changes of ownership, the shop, together with Tommy Dennis's old premises, was taken over in 1987 by a Punjabi family and all nine members help in the shop. They seem to have settled down as part of the Ashwell scene. We note that in September 1993 an estate agent, **Scott & Partners**, has opened in part of Tommy's old shop.

Going west just a bit farther, past Digswell Manor, originally the Manor of Westbury Nerneutes, in 1939 you would have come to **Bluegates Dairy**, started just after the First World War by Mrs Fordham. Ashwell milk was drawn from Ashwell cows, by the hands of Ashwell men, such as George Noble, and delivered by Neville Howes, Arthur Lambert and others. Horse drawn floats were replaced - Neville drove the first ever electric milk float from 1939. As he said in 1949, in a Broadcast to the Commonwealth, "The milk must go out 365 days a year, 366 in Leap Year"! But times change and, in 1969, Gurney Sheppard had the modern milking parlour and dairy built in Elbrook Lane and the milk drawn from the cows by Eastern Electricity. Due to modern methods of keeping milk fresh, Robert Sheldrick and Peter Greener now deliver the milk 260 days a year, but Ashwell's milk goes to a central bottling plant before it is distributed. Where Bluegates Dairy was is now Bacon's Yard.

Quality if not quantity

The south side of the High Street always had fewer shops than the north; by 1975 there were only two, albeit very important ones - **Days the Baker** and the Post Office. In 1939 there were eight and starting our survey for this time from west to east, we start with **A & C Christy** on the east corner of Bear Lane. The Christy empire occupied quite a large area between the High Street and Silver Street, the enterprises including a Newsagents Shop, Coal Merchants, and Mineral Water Manufacture, all well before 1939. Kirby Manor, the Christy's home, was part of the site. Mary Radford started in the Newsagents late in 1940, but war service very soon claimed Mary, who went to work on the land at Pepper's Farm, in Steeple Morden, earning 30/- per week. The foreman only gave her a week to survive the hard work but she stayed four years, during which she put on two stone and weighed eight stone at the end of the war! Nellie Christy soon had her back in the shop, where she worked until 1973.

The Neaves family took over the site in 1968, and in the early 70s sold part of it so a new Telephone Exchange could be built, replacing the more modest building in Alms Lane.

Bob Neaves was left a substantial sum of money, enabling him to finance his enterprises, but his lifestyle was too extravagant for the business he was doing. In the meantime, Australian Lindsay Colquhoun, living next door in Bear House, had started as the first ever resident village dentist (on a part-time basis) in part of the Surgery on the Church Lane side. Among his many amusing anecdotes, he tells of the occasion when he was treating a patient while his wife, Anne, was dealing with a queue at the Reception desk. A young man walked in, waited his turn patiently in the queue, and when he got to Anne told her that Bear House was on fire! Abandoning patients, Lindsay and Anne rushed along to Bear House, to be greeted by the Fire Engine and onlookers and the loud noise from a fiercely burning fire. Fortunately, the house was undamaged. A barn at the back was burnt down, the fire reputedly started by boys playing with matches. With Neaves' departure, Lindsay was able to open his practice where the Newsagents' shop had existed and where for 17 years until 1990 he looked, in his own phrase, in more mouths than possessed by the House of Commons. Lindsay also had been to prison more often than any Ashwell criminal - but his visits were always voluntary and in his professional capacity.

In the corner of The Rose & Crown yard, fronting on to the High Street, was the small brick building where shop repairer Les Worboys, a one-legged survivor of World War One, carried on his craft till after the Second World War.

Just past the Adelong, built in 1881 by a wealthy Ashwellian who made his fortune in Australia, is Ashwell's best known enterprise.

Day's the Ashwell bakers, were proclaimed Britain's best family baker in April 1989. The host of BBC2's food and drink programme, Michael Barry, himself a one-time bakery owner, said Day's seedy brown bread was absolutely delicious, but their success was due to the superb flavour and presentation of all their different types of bread. Joanna Smyth, who runs the bakery with the help of her aunts and, of course, her father and mother, was presented with the award by Georgina Holloway of the Flour Advisory Council.

Day's Bakery, with shops in Ashwell, Royston, Baldock and an outlet in Letchworth, employs some 40 people. Many different types of bread are made with a variety of flours from several suppliers and still moulded in the old-fashioned way by hand. Wedding, birthday and other celebration cakes are made and on sale, as are a variety of pastries, pork pies and sandwiches.

Before coming to Ashwell, Days had a bakehouse at Baldock in 1714. Then, a century later, they came to Ashwell, taking over a small bakehouse at Springhead - where there was, until about 1925, a pair of semi-detached cottages. Later, the family moved to the present site in High Street. They became the largest, and after 1956 the only, bakers in the village and at the beginning of this century, with sixteen children, also one of its largest families.

That Days the Bakers has become such a successful business is due entirely to the foresight, planning and hard work of Howard (who had served in the Fleet Air Arm during the war) and Hannah Day. They took the business over just after World War II, helped by Howard's father, Charles Day.

They thought that Ashwell should have something more than the average village bakers turning out tinned and cottage loaves, rock cakes and buns, with the occasional wedding cake, and that they had the ability to do it.

There was competition, not only from Lindsay's of Guilden Morden, who delivered regularly in Ashwell, but also from old Bob Kitchener, who came over from Hinxworth selling loaves from his pony and trap and, nearer still, the Co-op with their grocery shop facing Days. They also sent a baker's van round the village. One small bakery also existed in the village - Morley's, in West End, selling most of its bread by delivery to its customers. It closed in 1956.

Recalling some of Howard's early cake creations, there was a short cake figure with blobs of chocolate forming the eyes, nose and mouth, which sold for three old pence; then came the delicious pastry known as a jap. A very good recipe for a rich cake mix was devised for weddings, birthdays and other

High Street
L to R: pre-1939. *Two Brewers Pub, the cottage which is now Sue Birch Hairdressers, the Co-operative Society Shop, Turner's Garage, Fanny Adkins' shop, Jack Ashwell's Butcher's shop (late Eddie Brown's), Russells the Chemists, Westrope's house and shop. Old photograph greatly enlarged.* (Museum)

A summer's day in the High Street in 1964. L to R: *Eddie Brown's Butcher's Shop. Russells the Chemists, Westrope's and the recently restored Foresters' Cottages.* (Doris Shelton)

High Street, south side, 1964.
L to R: *1 Jessamine House, The Post Office, The Corner Shop, Winnie Stamford's Wool and Clothes Shop, now the Tea Shop, 31 High Street.* (Doris Shelton)

Barclays Bank plc moved here from a room in the Three Tuns in September 1974. See below.

Ashwell Post Office in 1940, on its present site. (Museum)

Searle's Top Shop (c. 1950) with Doris Thompson, centre and Mrs Searle (Byron's mother). Later Kingzett's and finally Collins' shop before becoming the Ashwell branch of Barclays Bank. (Museum)

celebrations. It was not exactly mass produced, but several slabs of this cake were always there maturing ready to be cut to size, iced and at the last moment decorated for the special occasion.

As the staff increased, so the bakery was extended and Brays, the builders, were kept busy building section after section further up the yard: new ovens, cold storage, cake preparation rooms etc and all the necessary equipment of a modern baker.

Incidentally, during the late 1920s, Mary Day, one of Howard's aunts, a smart and very efficient lady who wasted few words, served in the shop and when asked for half a dozen buns or rock cakes, they were in the bag with a quick flick of the wrist, into the customer's hands and sevenpence dropped in the till.

The Days were a very large family and as their living quarters were very cramped, Mary Day was in the habit of taking the metal bath Saturday evenings into the shop where she could bathe at her leisure away from the rest of the family. Somehow or other Jim Bonnett, the tailor, discovered Mary's secret and one dark night, before Ashwell had street lighting, Jim was seen kneeling on the steps of the baker's shop 'peeking' as old Ashwell people used to say, at Mary in all her glory. When Mary was told, she decided to get her revenge. The following Saturday evening she filled her bath as usual, made the water nice and soapy, then loaded a glass fountain pen filler from the bath and listened behind the shop door. At the usual time, Jim knelt on the step and had just put his eye to the keyhole when, quick as a flash, Mary squirted the soapy water into his eye. For a long time Jim dare not show his face in the village and brother Douglas was sent to collect the daily bread.

Bert Collis took over his father's shop opposite Turner's Garage in 1934. He preferred repairing bicycles to mending gramophones - you could never get the parts! - and didn't retire until 52 years later. In the Ashwell Show programme for 1948, he advertised 'A Perfect Cycle makes Perfect Safety and Cycling'. The Advertising Standards Authority might possibly have objected to his claim, 'All repairs by the District's best cycle mechanic', but undoubtedly he was a first class craftsman.

Where now stands the Beams and the two houses numbers 47 and 49 was originally a large pub known as The Bull's Head, pictured on the Dust Jacket of 'A different world ...'. **Ethel Dilley**, as an enterprising schoolgirl in the 1920s, sold apples and pears one August Bank Holiday out of a window of the Bull's Head where she lived, by then no longer a pub. Her stepfather had forgotten about the Bank Holiday when he had bought a load of fruit from Royston but Ethel sold the lot at sixpence a pound, and took £10.00 on the day. She then carried on for 6 weeks - the rest of her school holiday - and made enough money to buy herself a new coat and new pair of shoes. Even while she was at school (leaving at 14) she went up to Petticoat Lane on a Thursday with her stepfather to sell eggs while he sold live chickens to the Jews who came regularly to the market. She started her greengrocery and fruiterers' shop in Beams in the early 30s, selling her husband's produce - he had a few acres up Station Road. In 1940, with three children taking up too much time, she sold her shop to a Miss Ward, who later sold it to Mrs James. Mrs James was selling Wendy's Ices at 4d and 6d in 1948. In 1954 she was advertising Walls Ice Cream, Confectionery, etc and started a library for Home Lovers - presumably she rented out books like videos! The shop closed a bit later - television was getting popular, particularly after the 1953 Coronation, so perhaps not so many were reading books.

Winnie Stamford of Royston was looking for suitable shop premises in the 1930s and found them in Ashwell in part of the old Bull's Head site. One reason for coming was her friendship with members of the Waldock family. She opened her shop on the same day as Gurney Sheppard's mother was married - on 3 September, 1936.

At some time during her 34 years in Ashwell, Winnie moved to 31 High Street where from early 1992 in the Tea Rooms you can be served with lunch or delicious afternoon teas. Winnie Stamford retired in 1970. She had been helped in her shop by her two sisters, both of whom are still living, but Winnie passed away in 1986.

From 1972, No 31 was occupied by F A Flack & Co, who sold antique reproductions - furniture, mirrors, chandeliers etc, until the late seventies. In the eighties it was occupied for a short time by Liz Harris, also selling reproductions, by solicitors from London, Estate Agents, and from 1981-86, by Ashwell Delicatessen.

We finish our tour of retailers in the High Street at the building which in 1993 houses the **Post Office and Stores** and **Barclays Bank**. Up to her death in 1938, spinster Nellie Bryant (a seamstress and a keen member of the Zoar Strict Baptist Chapel) lived there, and we gather she bequeathed her house etc to Bert Gurney, the Chapel's Deacon. With the outbreak of war, Nellie Christy gave up the Post Office at the other end of High Street and Bert Gurney landed himself with the responsibility. He installed the appropriate staff, or rather inappropriate, as things went horribly wrong, and he ended up paying several hundreds of pounds to make up for the mistakes of his staff.

In the early 1950s, Mr & Mrs Moore ran the Post Office, and as an added attraction opened up the room where Nellie used to sit sewing in the light of a paraffin lamp, as the Singing Kettle Cafe. Morning Coffee, Afternoon Teas and Suppers were supplied, parties were catered for and - surprisingly - open all day Sundays. Bert Gurney was not at all pleased.

Later in the 50s, Mr & Mrs Proudfoot ran the Post Office, then in 1962 Jim Nicholson became Ashwell's Sub-Postmaster for 15 months, followed by Bill Wood. In 1967, Michael and Kay Richardson came from Luton to take over; they met at Limbury Baptist Church where Norman Gurney was choirmaster for fifteen years. They got engaged at midnight in the chapel porch after a Watchnight service.

John Thorpe, who followed them in May 1971, was a very different personality. Well known to quite a few Ashwell ladies because of his connections with the fruit farms of Bygrave and Gamlingay, he was not too happy with Post Office procedures. However, he was always a great help to his elderly customers who needed advice with their form filling. He was succeeded in December 1976 by the Paynes for two and a half years. Arthur and Betty Harris, in charge from 1979-86, must have been one of the most popular couples of all the occupants responsible for our Post Office services.

Kevan and Marion Morrison are with us in 1993, and Kevan has taken a great interest in Ashwell's history and memorabilia. He has published a highly colourful calendar for 1994 consisting of paintings by local artists of Ashwell.

For many years there was a shop next door to the Post Office, a tradition continued after the premises had stood empty for a year or so when **William Searle**, bought the shop premises, and advertised, 'All the year round with good class Fruit and Vegetables' and 'A good selection of sweets'. Mrs Searle, a very hardworking lady, served in the shop. William's father was choirmaster at the Methodist Chapel and his wife was the organist in the early 1900s. They had two sons, apart from William, one of whom was named Byron, who at the age of 18 was tragically killed in a road accident in the 1920s. Our contemporary Byron was named after him. In 1950, William decided to go into horticultural production, including pigs and poultry. But he gave teenager, Byron, the first lot of geese to kill for Christmas, as his son had become an experienced dispatcher of chickens. Pinning the first goose's neck under a crowbar, Byron pulled and heaved until it had a very long neck which seemed to stretch from here to eternity! It was also very dead. Later his father took on part-time work at Baldock and died at 77 in 1968. His widow survived him by 22 years, living until the age of 86.

The shop at Chapel Corner - another name for the turn from the High Street into Kingsland Terrace - was taken over by L B & I Glover who, in 1951, were trying to persuade Ashwellians to 'spend your sweet coupons with us' - a reminder that rationing was still with us in the 1950s - adding groceries to their stock and selling Meadowcream Ices. Wall's and Lyons certainly had no monopoly of ice cream - J Curtis in 'Bottom Searle's' was selling the Bestfood variety, and Mrs James, another High Street retailer, was promoting Wendy's Ices.

From 1953 to 1962, Zoe Kingzett, with husband, Robin, and family ran what was now called the Corner Stores, adding Cooked Meats to their range.

Daphne Collins and her husband, Arthur, took on the shop in the 1960s and were the last retailers there, closing down in 1974.

Barclays Bank for many years had had a room in the Three Tuns. The Hotel wanted their room back so Barclays sought more permanent accommodation. The Parish Council, in January 1974, was deeply concerned about the possibility of the Bank leaving the village. The shop at Chapel Corner became vacant, so all was well and Ashwell still had a Bank, open Monday to Friday, 10.00 am to 1.30 pm.

Mill Street shops

In 1939 Ashwell had three butchers - by 1975 the only survivor was **M V Crump** in Mill Street. Mark Crump, wounded in the First World War, struggled with ill health. The doctor ordered him to find a job in the country and after working in Letchworth, he bought the shop from the Bryant brothers - Ken and Marty - in the 1920s. There have, incidentally, been butchers in Mill Street for over 100 years.

In the depression of the late 20s and 30s, with four sons to bring up, he found it quite a struggle, made worse in the war by all four sons being called up;

rationing only added to the difficulties. **Philip** came back from the war in 1948 and took over in 1952. It has always been very much a family business, and two of Philip's sons, **Jonathan** and **David**, now run the business, which serves customers in a wide radius of Ashwell.

Philip has been doing a lot of research into the history of our butchers, and can trace them to the 18th century. In 1765, John Carter died and in the inventory of his Will it is clear that he had a slaughter house and a brew house, and from the description of the house itself it is most likely to be the last house in Swan Street, next to Gardiners Lane. Carter's Pond, opposite the Museum, may have some connection with him. Philip has logged at least 15 butchers named in the records of half of the nineteenth century.

Each Ashwell butchery had its own slaughter house pre-1939, but during the war meat was tightly rationed and Letchworth Bacon Factory tended to take the place of the individual slaughter house. Crumps only killed a few pigs, for individuals who were allowed to possess one or two on special permit. Norman Gurney can remember his father, who was in the cattle food trade anyway, keeping pigs which were slaughtered and cut into joints by Mark Crump. Philip had the Crump slaughter house demolished in 1955, building on the end accommodation for his parents joining on to the house next to the shop.

Ex-Japanese prisoner-of-war, **Bob Crump**, started a Wet Fish business when he came home in 1945, branching out into Fish and Chips in 1948, located in the Fire Service's Hut at the end of Swan Street. The Annual Parish Meeting of March 1948 records another refusal to grant a frying licence, but voted Bob its unanimous support. However, local custom was not sufficient, and the odd complaint about the cooking smells helped him to decide to move to Australia in 1951, where he has lived since - occasionally visiting Ashwell as he has this summer of 1993.

Terry Crump came back from the Army, after National Service, and carried on the **Wet Fish** business, visiting Ashwell every Thursday, until his final illness in 1989.

Mark Crump's other son, Ken, went into the Radio and Television business in Baldock's Hitchin Street, and sadly he passed away in 1990.

The Whitby Sisters

Having bought your meat supplies from Crumps and with a few minutes to spare, you walk further down Mill Street until you arrive at the Seven Springs Gallery, the unique creation of Marie and Pauline Whitby, daughters of those redoubtable Head Teachers of the Merchant Taylors' School, Geoffrey and Mabel Whitby, their successive terms running from 1933 to 1947, when the school was closed. In the 40s and 50s the Gallery was the Tailors' Shop, "Le Goodgroomes", where Jim and Doug Bonnett carried on their craft, and made some exceedingly good suits, some of which have lasted until now.

Marie, after her education at Hitchin Grammar School, taught for a time at Chesterfield Grammar School and for three years, from 1960, worked at the Old Vic Theatre as a scenic painter and property maker.

The opportunity to visit Ghana, where Pauline was working for the Food and Agriculture Organisation of the United Nations, enabled her to amass some capital, by making lino cuts depicting African life for the Ghana Arts Council. She sold a great deal of her work and with the capital she was encouraged to open her first shop in Ashwell, in Church Lane in 1964, on a part-time basis, teaching freelance while the business became established.

In 1972 she opened the Seven Springs Gallery in Mill Street, expanding her pottery-making as demand grew. Pigs were the most popular - thousands were produced, no two ever alike. At that time models of some 20 or more animals were being made. Since then, Marie has widened her products, multi-coloured medallions, chess men, figurines, buses and bas reliefs mounted on screen-printed hessian - a distinctive feature of Marie's work.

While the shop itself has attracted a wide clientele, selling to people who want hand crafted goods, many other craft workers have been able to find an outlet here - and to parents wanting simple and cheap toys for their children. As time progressed, the Barn backing on to Gardiners Lane has been put to excellent use as an Art Gallery, Exhibitions of Sculptures, Pottery, Woodwork, Tapestry and many other crafted items.

Marie as road sweeper

A frequent subject at Parish Council Meetings was the untidiness of Ashwell's Streets and its deposits of rubbish. There were constant complaints and members of the Women's Institute were so disgusted that, in 1969, they swept the High Street clean.

The Rural District Council supplied a Mechanical Road Sweeper in 1970 but it did not do a very good job. Even the extra litter bins were insufficient and more were frequently asked for.

Light dawned, however, in February 1971, when the Parish Council realised that regulations existed enabling Ashwell to have and pay for its own street cleaner.

But the pay of £12.00 a year did not attract any suitable applicants and for two more years we had to wait until Marie volunteered to do the job, in January 1973. A bit too late, a Mr Coone applied for the position, but he was under the mistaken impression that accommodation went with it! Anyway, Marie got on with it - from the account she sent us of her experiences.

"In 1973 there seemed to be more and more rubbish on the streets; the Parish Council had only £12.00 a year to pay a street cleaner, (the District Council at that time not permitting the rates to be increased for this purpose) so naturally could not find one. I wrote to the Parish Council and asked for the job. They accepted and gave me a cart, solid iron, large and heavy (even when not full of wet rubbish). I allotted two hours on Monday and Friday mornings, and managed to get round the High Street, Back and Silver Streets and Mill Street, and each week also cleaned up one particularly bad spot elsewhere. It was a very sociable job, everyone stopped for a chat, so that the two hours stretched considerably. On the whole, people approved of my efforts, which were entirely for my own satisfaction as I hated seeing the village messy. I did get attacked (verbally) twice for encouraging the local youths to throw down their papers and cans for me to pick up!

"When I applied, the Royston Crow reported the fact briefly, and because the Women's Lib thing was much in the news at the time, the rest of the local press picked it up. Reporters began to appear, wanting to take my picture with the cart. Then both channels of TV came along to film me for the local news. One man actually lay down in the road in front of me, on a steep slope, so as to get a worm's eye view; as the cart was full, I had some difficulty in preventing it from running over him! I began to feel slightly harried, but thought anything that drew attention to the litter problem must be good, so went along with it.

"I did it for three years before sciatica and rheumatism got so uncomfortable that I found it difficult to push the cart, when full, to the dump behind Bear House (now the Housing Association's Housing Estate). I asked the Parish Council for a lighter cart in order to be able to carry on. (I had my eye on the natty little yellow ones used by the street cleaners in Hitchin and Letchworth.) They eventually came up with a dustbin on a golf trolley; light, certainly, but I had to do three trips to collect the same amount of rubbish! "Meanwhile, I was getting busier in the shop, and found it more difficult to find time, so eventually I fizzled out. Shortly afterwards the Parish Council was allowed to offer reasonable pay for a sweeper and obtained one, so all was well."

Marie does not say so, but she donated her earnings towards the PTA Fund for a School Swimming Pool, and later for the Church Tower Restoration Fund. A noble effort.

Sister, Pauline, is not only an avid reader; she is also a notable writer of Science Fiction having had over ten stories published, three of them in anthologies and one book published. Part of her earlier career has already been mentioned.

Marie became more involved on the manufacturing side so Pauline concentrated on the Shop and Gallery. In the shop was always a magnificent tabby cat - there are five altogether, wandering about the premises. The shop itself is now run by Elaine Pym.

Ashwell Doctors (AS)

How well the Ashwell Surgery, built on the site of an old cattle shed, blends in with its green surroundings in Lawyers Close, Gardiners Lane, with its pleasant reception area and well planned surgeries, opened in 1990. From 1953 in the busy High Street, the Surgery had been sited in the shop where from way back in the last century Fanny Adkins and her family had sold watches and clocks, stockings and gloves, button-sided boots and iron pattens to strap under the boots in muddy weather, and many more. We thought this was a grand place but wondered whether Fanny would have approved of all these sick, lame, halt and blind people, naked and half naked, being injected and probed by doctors and nurses, even in her sitting room.

The surgery before that, in 1950, was lower down the High Street, in the old Saddlery, where the Ashwell photographers, Ian and Sue Walters, now live, and towards the end of the 1940s Arthur Lambert (of the Brethren Assembly) repaired shoes, taking over from harness maker, Bill Trudghill, who in turn took over from Sam Radford, Mary Radford's grandfather.

During the 18th century, Ashwell relied on outside medical men. Doctors Kintish, Savage, Webster, Barnby, Ellard, Nunn, Hix and Hicks until 1820, when Dr Charles Woodforde became the first resident doctor, followed in 1826 by Dr Laroux; and in 1829 by Dr Tyndale, who lived at the house then known as Fairview (now Spring House, opposite the Springs). On 3 June 1843, at a meeting of the Loyal Egbert Lodge of the Independent Order of Oddfellows held at the Bull's Head Inn (opposite Plait Hall in the High Street), Brother Edward Tyndale M R C S and Vice-Grand Master of the Lodge, was appointed its medical attendant. Dr Tyndale resigned in 1880, died in 1883, and was followed by Dr Swinson, whose archer's bow can be seen in the Museum. Then surprise, surprise, Ashwell had, in the late 19th century, a black doctor, Doctor Johnson. My father, who was born in 1884, told me of a black doctor but I could not find any information about him until I was invited to visit Doctors John and Sheila Moynihan at their home at Guilden Morden, to which they had retired. There, in their spacious lounge, whilst a hedgehog ambled silently across the lawn, Dr John told me about Dr Johnson, Ashwell's black doctor, who became insane and went on the rampage smashing windows in the High Street; and was probably taken to the Three Counties Asylum at Arlesey.

Dr R E H Woodforde came to Ashwell in 1900, taking over the previous doctor's house, now known as Spring House. Dr Woodforde planned to build a red brick house in the Georgian style next to Fairview, where the bungalow named Oversprings now stands; but when Baileys the builders sent my grandfather, John Sheldrick, to dig the trenches, he could not find a foundation solid enough to support the weight of the house. It is believed from the present level of the Springs basin that the land sloped up to Ashwell Street until roughly 200 years ago when, after much filling and consolidating, the present road was made. Eventually the builders found, higher up the slope, a solid base on which to build; but, said Dr John with a smile, "Here they found another snag, three walnut trees"! Instead of removing any of the trees, the plans were re-drawn and the house was made smaller, which resulted in the very small surgery which older Ashwellians will remember, and which I dealt with in the previous book. The house named The Mount, now Ashwell House, was built in 1904. Dr Woodforde retired to Somerset in 1933; but before he left he warned his successor to collect the fallen walnuts before morning surgery at 8.30 am or, he said, the patients will have them.

At eighteen years of age, John Moynihan decided to become a doctor and studied medicine at King's College, London, where he met his future wife. Later, as senior registrar at Charing Cross Hospital, he followed medicine and modern surgery and did as much research as his spare time would allow.

Doctor Sheila went on from King's College to Queen's Hospital, Dalston for sick children, where she made a study of the illnesses which afflict children; in fact, she became an authority on children's ailments of all kinds. When she and Doctor John decided to find a country practice in which to raise their family, her knowledge proved of great value, not only to the children of Ashwell but to a great part of North Herts.

Until the changeover was completed, Dr Woodforde introduced Dr John to his patients, not only at the surgery twice daily (only once on Tuesday and Sunday) but also on visits to the patients.

Not more than half a dozen patients attended each surgery, but the doctor was expected to make up to 30 visits a day. Dr Woodforde's charge for one visit, plus one bottle of medicine, was 3s.6d and for a repeat bottle of medicine 1s.6d. Gwenda Westrope, who was Ashwell and District Nurse from 1925 until her marriage to Charles Westrope in 1931, has told me of her work as midwife, school nurse and health visitor, pushing her bicycle round Hinxworth, Caldecote, Newnham, Wallington, Slip End and Odsey, attending the sick and delivering babies by lamp light or even candles. (Electricity only came to Ashwell in 1930).

On coming to Ashwell, Dr Sheila had retired to bring up the family, but in late 1936 there was a severe outbreak of 'flu, which involved Dr Sheila helping in the practice, visiting patients and dispensing enormous numbers of bottles of medicine.

Dr Sheila pioneered the Ashwell Infant Welfare Centre in 1937, the first of its kind in Hertfordshire. It was opened in the Congregational Church Hall with all the necessary equipment paid for by the doctor and her committee of voluntary helpers, both directly and through fund raising activities. It may not be fully appreciated that pre-1939, large families were brought up in real poverty, when many children went hungry and malnutrition meant rickets and similar ailments.

Although the war brought not only more problems and more children with the influx of some 100 evacuees, rationing encouraged a more equitable distribution of food and the government helped by the free supply of vitamins. Additionally, the clinic sold various vitamin-filled preparations. Dr Sheila pointed out that due to the scarcity of milk, oranges and vitamins, it was absolutely essential to make good such defects.

The clinic's sterling work greatly influenced the future treatment of children and nowadays there is a network of such clinics all over the country.

Ashwell's continued first in the Further Education Centre from 1947, twice monthly, and from June 1990 in the new surgery.

It was early in 1941 that Dr John was taken ill with a severe chest complaint and Dr Sheila took over the practice. Dr John was treated initially at the Brompton Hospital, London, during the blitz, and subsequently at Papworth. Then a hut was built in the garden where the two doctors slept, so he could get plenty of fresh air.

Dr Sheila was appointed Assistant Medical Officer for North Herts in 1948, responsible for several clinics, and was then able to make full use of her earlier studies and training at Queen's Hospital. So with injections, inoculations and vaccinations she fought a war against the scourges of whooping cough, tetanus, measles and the dreaded poliomyelitis, though there was quite a lot of opposition from people who disagreed with such measures.

In 1973, after 40 years of caring for the medical needs of Ashwell and District, Doctors John and Sheila retired. As Parish Councillors and members of every worthwhile committee, they had been deeply involved at every level of village life. In 1978, Dr John accepted the Presidency of the newly formed Horticultural Society and with Dr Sheila continues to take a great interest in its very successful activities.

In 1975 the full team of doctors were Dr Kenneth Heaton, Dr Martin Hoffman and Dr Fergus Moynihan, carrying on the family tradition.

The hedgehog had long since completed its morning stroll across the lawn and disappeared into the bushes when it was time for me to say goodbye to the two doctors, whom I first met nearly 60 years ago.

Some of the early residents of Wolverley House take it easy in the lounge, during the 1970's.
L to R: *Mrs Oyston, Mrs. Knight, Mrs. Gray, Mrs. Pidgeon, Mrs. Bullock and Mrs Lawrence.*
(N. Herts Gazette/G. Berry)

Above: *Before Bacon's Yard. From Dixies Meadow to Christy's Corner. L to R: Dixies Cottage, Cambridge villas, The Saddlery, the remainder of the old Dairy, the thatched cow shed has gone, but black and white cows can be seen; V.G. Stores and the Butcher's shop.* Top right: *Wolverley House.* Centre front: *Bear House (1976)* (Mrs. L. MacBeth)

Below: *Wolverley House: Homes for Senior Citizens, designed by Donald Insall and Partners for North Herts District Council in 1973 on the former Bury kitchen gardens in Gardiners Lane* (Gurney Sheppard)

Ashwell in Council

Ashwell's Parish Council, which had 12 members meeting quarterly in 1939 (from July 1951 it met monthly), elected by an open vote at the Annual Parish Meeting held normally every March, played an important role in village affairs. During the war, it is clear that its scope for action was very limited. Various projects were put on one side, but at least in November 1939 the Cemetery Chapel, designed by Sir Albert Richardson, had been completed.

In April 1939, £4 was spent on the Tennis Courts on the Recreation Ground, and during the ensuing years the 'Rec' was the subject of much discussion - how to keep it tidy, prevent the trees being a danger and when could we have a new pavilion. Better equipment and dedicated workers have solved the first problem, Dutch Elm disease destroyed the trees, and the new pavilion was eventually opened in 1960 - the story is told elsewhere - but had to have a lot of improvement in the early 1970s.

Having acquired a Cemetery Chapel, its maintenance and that of the Burial Ground were a constant source of concern. In 1943 there were complaints about the Caretaker's work. Perhaps he didn't like the lawn mower, bought in 1940 from Brookers for £2 4s.10d. In 1944 he asked for 1/6d an hour, which was refused, and later in the year he resigned. The new caretaker was paid 2/- an hour and we note that the old mower was replaced in 1951 with one which cost £50! We ought to mention that half the Parish Clerk's salary at that time, small as it was, was paid for work done in connection with the Cemetery. A lot of time had to be spent in council revising the Burial Ground Fees.

Street lighting was a perennial subject. All the lights went out over Ashwell during the war but afterwards the cost, additional lights and repairs to lights were frequently discussed. In 1939, the North Metropolitan Electricity Company was responsible for our electricity supplies and they cost £70 a year. By 1975, by which time the Eastern Electricity Board has taken over, the cost was nearer £1,000.

Road conditions were constantly on the agenda: their safety, their state of repair and their untidiness. Short Bear Lane was made one way, but the roundabout suggested for the crossroads of Silver and Back Streets with Bear Lane was not achieved. The state of the roads, both those in the village and approaching it, was often described as filthy and disgusting. The Rural District Council did not seem cooperative. Litter bins were requested but were tardy in arriving and then they didn't suit. Keeping the roads clean in the village seemed an insurmountable problem. Marie Whitby came to the rescue in 1973 but the pantomime-like efforts to supply her with a suitable barrow she tells in an earlier chapter. Thankfully in 1993 we have Fred Moule to keep our streets clean.

In 1948 there were calls for the collection of household refuse to be made weekly, not fortnightly and this subject came up from time to time. Twenty years later our Rural District Councillor said that he understood the cost of a weekly collection would be prohibitive. But our councillors kept pressing the matter, and in 1973 were successful, and ever since we have had weekly collections.

The Village Hall was another perennial subject. We deal with it in more detail elsewhere, but suffice to say that it caused many headaches both inside and outside the Council.

Relations with Hitchin Rural District Council were never easy, particularly regarding planning matters. Planning authorities after the war frequently acted in an arrogant manner, ignoring local opinion. Even so, the battle to gain proper consultation at a local level, even after the efforts of both Council and the Ashwell Association in the 70s, has always to be fought, as was evidenced so clearly in the controversy about the Airey houses in 1992.

During our period, for all but three years we were served by only two Parish Clerks - **Madge Howes**, 1941-64, reputed to be the first ever lady Parish Clerk, and **David Billson**, 1965-78.1975 was a watershed year in the Council's history. Five major stalwarts, who had served Ashwell for many years, resigned. Ashwell was to be fortunate in that those who took their places shared their ideals of community service and their dedication to it.

Marking the retirement of five Parish Councillors. **Seated:** *Geoffrey Coad, John Bray, Howard Day, all retiring.* **Standing:** *Clerk to the Council David Billson, Sam Wallace, Eric Gurney. Liz Moynihan, Jeremy Fordham, Carol Moore, Philip Crump and Gurney Sheppard, 1975. Eric Gurney and Philip Crump were the other two retiring.* (Eric Gurney)

Ashwell at Prayer

When that tough little parson, Reverend Panajotti Webb, Ashwell's Rector from 1892 to 1925, lambasted his congregation in his Sunday morning sermon, sparing the feelings of none from the lowliest to the wealthiest, and reserving his greatest wrath for the shopkeepers, he invariably was addressing a large and wide cross-section of the village community; his counterparts in the other churches, whose members he despised as heretics on the way to hell, may not have been quite so robust in their sermonising but the Congregational, Methodist and, to a lesser extent, the Strict Baptists were well supported.

The Brethren

In 1939 there were five places of worship. A few will remember the Brethren, who met in the old Co-op Hall in Swan Street. A prominent member was George Noble, for a long time Dairyman at the old Bluegates Dairy. George, living in Baldock in 1993, still actively practises his Christian faith at the age of 88, regularly visiting patients nearly every day in our local hospitals. His late wife, Margaret, played the harmonium for the services. Another leading worshipper was Arthur Lambert, who also had a close connection with milk as he was a door-to-door milkman before and during World War II for George Longley's Dairy in Station Road, now the site of Sunnymead Orchard mobile homes. Unlike another milkman, Neville Howes, who was strongly agnostic, if not an atheist, Arthur, with his gentle and ever-smiling wife Kathleen, was always ready to hand out religious tracts and spread the Gospel. The Brethren's services, which were very much modelled on those of the 'Plymouth Brethren', were simple and unritualistic. The morning service was known as 'Breaking of Bread', when any man, providing he was a believer, could speak, read the Scripture or choose a hymn, the meeting ending with communion. Evening was 'The Gospel' Meeting and was held with a visiting speaker. During its heyday 40 to 50 children attended its Sunday School, including Albert Sheldrick's daughter, Susan.

By 1975 membership had declined and without new blood the Ashwell meeting was closed down in the early 1980s.

Zoar Strict Baptist Chapel

When the publisher's father, Bert Gurney, and his family came to Ashwell in 1932, 'Zoar' Strict Baptist Chapel in Gardiners Lane was in a sorry state of repair. Few attended although these included the well known village tailor, Mr Bonnet, and his wife who played the harmonium until 3 September, 1939 (see 'A Different World', page 52), and the Shelton family. Mary Bryant and her brother, Septimus, who lived in one of the Workhouse Cottages in Swan Street, were regular attenders.

Mary dressed very soberly in a brown serge outfit, her full length skirt and helmet-like hat amusing the Gurney children, while old Septimus scandalised other members of the congregation by going to the Rose and Crown for his pint of beer after morning service. The Chapel, built in 1854 by Joseph Flitton with Stotfold stock bricks and slated roof, was re-decorated in the early 30s throughout and services were held again in the Chapel instead of the little vestry at the back. When, in 1954, Zoar's Centenary was celebrated, the Chapel was in very good decorative order, but the hard wooden pews were unchanged. As in most churches which practise baptism by total immersion, the chapel had a Baptistry, which was a rectangular structure, sunk into the floor, large enough for two people to stand in, the depth of water when a person was baptised being 3 feet. Bert Gurney's wife was the first person to be baptised in the re-opened sanctuary, on a freezing cold night - 20 degrees Farenheit - in January 1936, the night King George V died. Although the water was equally cold, Gladys, in the joy of the occasion, never felt its coldness! Up to 1973, the services were conducted by itinerant ministers. From that year to the present time, Robert Field of Steeple Morden has been the Pastor. Strict Baptist Services were basically very simple - the same format is used today. Three hymns, a scripture reading, an extempore prayer which invariably lasted at least 15 minutes, and usually included everything from the sinful state of mankind to reverent prayer for the Royal Family. Inevitably there was much repetition and we counted one minister using the phrase 'Dear Lord' 50 times in his prayer. How we longed for him to use an alternative form of addressing the Almighty just to relieve the tedium. The sermon which followed lasted up to an hour - $^3/_4$ minimum - and was preached with no notes - anathema to these sober minded Calvinists who depended entirely on the Holy Spirit for their message. None was trained in public speaking or went to any theological college; sometimes they spoke so quietly they could hardly be heard, others frequently shouted denunciations from the high pulpit.

Occasionally the old stove, fuelled by coke, which in cold weather had to be lit early on Sunday morning, would explode, filling the Chapel with fumes. One somewhat eccentric attender was Frank Noble, who for many years was an instructor at the Ascot Training Centre in Letchworth, a highly intelligent man from Bygrave, who with his wife lived eventually in Springhead. He had quite a lot to do with the design of the ill-fated R101 Airship and was due to go on her maiden voyage when he was forced to make way for a VIP. The R101 crashed in France, killing all its passengers. Frank, however, survived to tell the tale, into the 1980s. During a service, if he had to go up to the front of the Chapel, he always walked backwards down the long aisle on his return to the back, a reverential manoeuvre adding a spark of interest to the proceedings.

Strict Baptists, as their named implies, were strict in many respects, not least in their relations with other church goers. Bert Gurney, Deacon from 1932 to 1958, had a wider perspective for which other members of the denomination criticised him, and even boycotted the Chapel. He always took part in the 'Days of Prayer' during the Second World War. United Services were held in the Parish Church to pray for victory and peace. All the churches took part, the church was crowded, and Bert would read one of the lessons.

Above: *Rev. Arthur Perkins, long- serving Pastor at the Congregational Church until 1943.* (Dorothy Andrews)

Above: *The old Co-op Hall was the meeting place of the Assembly of Brethren.* (George Noble)

Centre: *The interior of the Methodist Church built in 1880. Demolished in 1979.* (A. Sheldrick)

Left: *Members of the Mothers Union in the 1950's.* (Mrs. B. Wallace)

Members of the Ashwell Wesleyan Methodist Chapel attend a dinner to celebrate the 80th birthday of their well known local preacher Silas Worboys. (1941)
(Dorothy Roberts)

Members of the Ashwell Wesley Guild who entertained at a 1930's Methodist Garden Party at The Elms then the home of Miss L. Bryant. Wilfred Bryant, Miss Bryant's father, was the partner in the wheelwrights' business, Bryant and Worboys. (Dorothy Roberts)

Before 1939, every woman attending church wore a hat. To help the war effort, in a rather obscure sort of way, this rule was relaxed by mainstream church authorities, but Strict Baptist ladies to this day continue the practice. One serious side effect, of course, was the mortal damage done to the hat trade in Luton, with which Plait Hall in the High Street had close connections. But if these pious ladies wore hats, they were also not allowed to speak or pray in any service.

At the end of our period, Zoar Chapel was reasonably well supported but more of its regular congregation came from outside the village, and the same applies in 1993.

From Congregational to United Reformed

What is now the United Reformed Church was, in 1939, known as the Congregational. It had its own Manse in Kingsland Road, and its full-time Pastor for twenty years had been Reverend Arthur Perkins. It was said that he was a very clever man and interested in astronomy. Some members thought he was too academic. He was a little man, who took very short steps and wore a black felt hat and a Sherlock Holmes type of coat with a sort of cape across the shoulders. Mrs Perkins, a very smartly dressed lady, who spoke in a high pitched squeal of a voice, was one of those dithering ladies who would faint at the sight of a mouse. When she was annoyed with the Sunday School scholars, however, her voice became very deep.

Daughter Francesca, who died a few years ago in London, was a delicate flower, but was also a fine musician who gave music lessons to Ashwellians, including Norman Gurney.

After Reverend Perkins died in 1943, there was a two-year interregnum until Reverend Herbert Hard became Pastor. His wife was also a very smart dresser, but they were a much more down to earth couple, and soon accepted in the life of the village. After 6 years they left, due to Mr Hard's ill-health, and for the first time for many years a part-time Lay Pastor was appointed - Mr J Griffiths - who was very popular, especially with the young people. However, numbers were declining, as in so many churches. The Griffiths' pastorate ended in 1959 and eventually, in 1961, Fred Sillence, then Editor of the Royston Crow, was appointed Pastor, a position he has held with distinction and devotion ever since. In 1991 there was a wonderful celebration of his 30 years of service.

In 1972, by a majority vote, the church agreed to affiliate to the new United Reformed denomination, formed out of a union of the Presbyterian and Congregational Denominations, and in 1977 support for the chapel was boosted considerably when the Methodist Chapel closed. Mary Radford, a life-long member of the Congregational Church - she was christened by Reverend Arthur Perkins - contrasts the cooperation between the Parish Church and the URC in the 80s and 90s compared with previous generations, recalling in particular the attitude of pre-1939 Rector F H J Newton, who liked to be known as Father Newton, a high churchman with strong Anglo-Catholic tendencies, who was most intolerant of the Nonconformists. When the Annual Remembrance Service was held, he allowed no other denomination to take part. To counteract this the Methodists and Congregationalists held their own services in the Maltings.

Intolerance breeds intolerance and Strict Baptist, Bert Gurney, for whom anything that smacked of Catholicism or otherwise was an abomination, would not permit his daughter, Joyce, to attend the weekly service at the Merchant Taylors' School, conducted by the Reverend Father! Times change, and one of his most welcome visitors during his last illness, twenty or so years later in 1958, was Reverend Jack Catterick, who said in his sermon at the time, "If you want to know how a Christian should die, go and see Bert Gurney".

As has been mentioned previously, Reverend Panajotti Webb, in spite of being a low churchman, had also been antagonistic towards Nonconformists, and certainly had little time for Reverend Perkins. However, he was quite friendly with his predecessor, Reverend William Morgan, who, he was delighted to announce after the latter had ended his pastorate in 1919, had been converted - to the Church of England!

From devotions to demolition

In 1939, the Methodist Church in the High Street, an imposing edifice built in 1880, was a prosperous part of the church-going community. It never had its own Pastor but was a member church of the Biggleswade Circuit. It had some outstanding leaders - Silas Worboys, Alf Brown, Lily Bryant, Annie Hyslop, Eddie Brown, who were supported by good congregations.

One by one these died and were not replaced. Dedicated people like Douglas and Millie Harradine, Ivy and Eddie Brown, carried on for a time. But the ravages of anno domini were also causing havoc to the church building. A lot of money was needed and was not forthcoming. So in 1978 the building was sold to Mr Tom Griffin who bought it, he said, for the village. But his altruism could not be maintained. No one quite knew what to do with the building and, having come under the auctioneer's hammer, it disappeared under that of the demolisher's.

Twenty-five members joined the United Reformed Church, thus adding much valued strength to that church.

The records of the Methodist Church are somewhat scanty. Someone is needed to research its history and write it down before it is too late.

Church of England

One of Bessie Wallace's favourite Rectors was Reverend Henry Allday Griffith, and although he's a bit outside our period, succeeding the pugnacious Panajotti Webb, the circumstances of his coming were so remarkable and his organisational ability was put to such good use, he succeeded in a remarkable way in renovating the church fabric and having the rectory cut down to size and modernised. His predecessor, who had little interest in such matters, had allowed the church to become dangerous and the interior of the church was dark and dank.

But when in 1925 Henry Griffith left South Africa where he had been Archdeacon of Pretoria, he was coming home to his beloved Wales to die, having been diagnosed as having an incurable cancer and was already too weak to stand without support. During the lengthy sea voyage he seemed to recover, and was able to walk off the ship unassisted. Back in Wales he made a miraculous recovery, and very soon his friend (and colleague in South Africa), now Bishop of St Albans, told him, "You can't rot down there. I've got a job for you in Ashwell"! It was a job he was to do extremely well and his national appeal for money to fund the major repairs needed to put the church in order immensely benefited future generations. His 1934 successor, Reverend F H J Newton was a very different character - (see 'A Different World' page 83) remembered possibly as much for his prodigious ability to consume large quantities of beer as for his theological inclinations.

Bessie Wallace's father, John Sale, was the longest serving People's churchwarden this century, from 1902 to 1957, and was re-elected on a parishioner's proposal at every Annual Meeting to the end of this remarkable period of service. One outstanding feature of village life has been the number of men and women who have devoted so much of their time and talents to serve their chosen church or chapel as the Anglican prayer has it: 'Without asking for any reward save that of knowing that we do Thy will'. In our account of church life, we may emphasise the role played by the 'professionals' but while it would be impossible to name individuals, John Sale epitomises the need each church has for lay people to carry on, whoever the incumbent, and sometimes, in spite of! If John Sale had to suppress his essentially low church approach during the reign of Father Newton, when Reverend Henry James Edgar Chew was Rector from 1938-1941, he had to cope not only with the man but also his mother, who was of a domineering disposition. However, he was to have even more to cope with. After one Sunday Evensong, James Chew said goodnight in the normal way to John Sale, and then disappeared from rectory and village without trace. His distraught Mother rang John to ascertain if he had said anything or appeared in any way unusual the night before, as he had not come home. Mr Chew never reappeared in Ashwell. In 1943 he resurfaced as Vicar of Ravensthorpe and other nearby villages in the Diocese of Peterborough and stayed there until 1956.

Then came Reverend Henry Martindale, a very popular parson but he, unlike Mr Chew, had a wife who was also well liked. She started the Young Wives' Group which any young wife could join, whether church or not, unlike the Mothers' Union, an official church organisation to be found in many parishes, then and now.

In a way, Henry came to Ashwell to recuperate both physically and mentally after a heart attack, brought about, it was said, after a bruising confrontation with the Duke of Bedford, a somewhat mentally unbalanced eccentric, who unceremoniously turfed him out of the Woburn benefice, which was in the Duke's gift. Henry Martindale served Ashwell during the war but another heart attack in 1946 was one too many and he was buried in Ashwell Cemetery, mourned by many. He had been a uniting influence in the parish, especially in his relationships with the other churches.

A knowledgeable Ashwellian (we think Miss Anne Hyslop, 24 years Headmistress of Ashwell School till 1941) wrote a book entitled 'Ashwell : A Short Local History' in 1950 or thereabouts. In a touching tribute to Henry Martindale she writes : "During the years of his ministry in Ashwell he had come to love the village, and the village people had come to love him. He was able to earn the esteem of all, from the Bishop down to little children. His great lifework was the spread of the Gospel and the fulfilment of 'Thy Kingdom Come'. Our hearts go out to Mrs Martindale and we ask that God in His infinite compassion may be her strength and stay".

The Reverend John F B Keith, fresh out of the Army and a young married man, succeeded the gentle Martindale. This extremely able individual was a very different kettle of fish. Forthright in his views, he got himself into trouble when he mixed religion with politics, comparing a nationalised industry with Hitler's National Socialism. His comments were pounced upon by the National Press.

In a more attractive vein, his revival of a Rogationtide Service in 1948 was reported in a National Daily - The News Chronicle - as follows: "A revival of the age-old custom of a Rogationtide Service took place today in this village from which springs the Cam.

From the fourteenth-century church the Rector, Rev J F B Keith, led a congregation of 40 (men, women, children and babes in prams) round the farms in the parish and blessed the crops, farmyards, gardens, orchards, streams and meadows. In a meadow surrounded by tall poplar trees Mrs Wolverley Fordham, who owns the land, read a short prayer and Mr Keith gave the blessing.

Similar prayers, all uttered by the farmers on whose ground the congregation was meeting, were said, in an orchard where a dozen bullocks stood silently watching, in a cornfield where the crop already looked green and sturdy, on the tiny green by a long-closed village prison and in a farmyard amid newly whitewashed buildings.

And finally in the churchyard, sweet-scented May blossom, where the verger, Mr Percy Sheldrick, recited the prayer: '... prosper in their labours our farmers and fruitgrowers, dairymen, gardeners and beekeepers, that they, ministering to the bodily needs of Thy people, may themselves be rewarded in body and soul." In the previous year, villagers had witnessed nature in one of its more violent moods when gales caused much damage to the church spire; some of the sheet lead was torn off and the iron post on which the weathercock revolved was broken, causing the weathercock to be catapulted into the adjoining meadow, together with the large glass marble which acts as a ball bearing on which the cock revolves. The bird, which is made from sheet copper, was badly buckled.

When he was a schoolboy in the early 1920s, Albert Sheldrick had heard two schoolboys boasting that their grandmothers had sat on the weathercock. He writes:

"I tried to picture either Liza Winters, Ted Chandler's grandma or Mrs Billy 'Roundarse', Jack Geeves' grandma, sitting up there 176 feet above ground level astride the cockerel, as though they were riding on Jim Harris's flying horses, their skirts billowing out in the wind, showing their red flannelette bloomers. Of course the boys were pulling our legs. Years later, it must have been about 1946, when the account book cum diary of the Bacon family (harness-makers, rope-makers, churchwardens and Ashwell worthies) had been saved from a bonfire and brought to the Museum, I read - '1863: Great rejoicing here in commemoration of the marriage of the Prince of Wales, the weathercock knocked off in erecting the flag. Repaired and re-gilt by Mr Hoye. Ladders erected on Monday 29 June, weathercock put back by Tom Eversden by 7 o'clock morning of 30 June.'"

Rogation Sunday 1948. The Rector Rev. John Keith, the choir and parishioners bless the Whitby farmyard. (Mrs. B. Wallace)

Parishioners assemble in the churchyard on Saturday 27th, 1966 before boarding coaches to attend Westminster Abbey's 900th Anniversary, at which Percy Sheldrick presented a cushion which he had embroidered specially for the occasion: "One God One People". (Herts. Pictorial/Museum)

So the crafty old women, schoolgirls at the time, really had sat on the weathercock, either in the churchyard or in Mr Hoye's workshop, before it was put back on the spire.

But back to 1947 and Albert continues -

"After we had erected the necessary scaffolding, Sir Albert Richardson, the church architect, climbed the tower staircase and went on to the scaffolding to examine the lead and the timbers below. We removed the rest of the lead and dropped it over the tower parapet, from where it was taken away to be re-cast and later replaced by Messrs Norman Underwood of Leicester. The spire rises 26ft above the tower and is constructed of three or maybe four oak trees roughly erected in the shape of a tripod, then clad with boarding on which the lead was dressed.

I was surprised to find that it was possible to rock the whole spire about an inch in any direction.

The lead was replaced, and on the base of the spire there is a dedication to the memory of Colonel Eustace Hill and his son, Squadron Leader Anthony Eustace Hill, DSO, DFC, the latter killed in the Second World War. Jim Roberts, Bray's plumber, re-shaped the weathercock. (It would be interesting to know whether the bullet holes we discovered in it were made by American, British or German airmen.) The bird was re-gilded by Mr Skeels of Letchworth, paid for by Fred Bray, and early in March 1948, after filling the socket with grease and replacing the marble, Fred and I lowered it on to the spindle."

All this had cost a great deal of money and the Annual Horse Show, Gymkhana and Summer Fair, as it was called in 1948, had as its chairman Reverend Keith and was in aid of the Church Spire Restoration Fund.

Reverend F Keith's somewhat eventful ministry ended in his departure to Fakenham where he continued in the ministry until he and his family emigrated to New Zealand where he had two brothers. There he had a distinguished ecclesiastical career, ending up as Canon and Precentor of Christchurch Cathedral. He died in 1991.

The very able Reverend Keith was followed for a short time by Reverend Geoffrey Oakeshott, whose ministry, lasting only two years to 1953, was too brief to make much of a mark on Ashwell, especially as he was plagued by ill-health.

Reverend Jack Catterick

"He had the warmth of a Tynesider, the sensitivity of a musician and the determination of a benevolent bulldozer." Thus did Archbishop Runcie, preaching at Festal Evensong at the 40th Anniversary of the Ashwell Festival, describe Reverend Jack Catterick. He intended to stay for just a few years but held the living for 24 until forced by throat cancer in 1977 to retire. He made a remarkable recovery from a heart attack in 1974, and after retirement made a partial recovery from cancer. He died in 1983.

In the intervening years, Jack made a very active contribution to village life. Not content with being a parson, he played a vital rôle in many village activities. Like Reverend Keith, he became Chairman of the Horse Show and Gymkhana within a year, a position he held for 4 years. The 1954 Show was in aid of Ashwell, Hinxworth and Newnham Village Halls, Newnham Church and its Methodist Church, now the Village Hall. These were some of the objects of the Show fundraising while he was chairman.

The Show of 1956 also announced - 'Ashwell Church is 600 years old. The

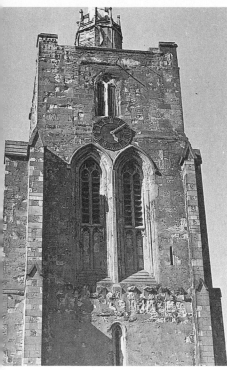

A 1947 picture of the Church Tower.
(Museum)

Rev. John J. Catterick, Rector from
1953-1977. (Anthony Catterick)

Rev. Frank Pickard, after
working for Johnson
Matthey of Royston for
several years, trained for
the ministry. Was vicar of
Old Warden, Beds 1968-
1973 and Priest in charge
of Hinxworth, Newnham
and Edworth 1973-1986.
In 1986 Frank and his wife
Mary retired to Norfolk.
(Rev. Frank Pickard)

The interior of Ashwell Parish Church 1947. (Museum)

village people have raised nearly £3,000 - another £2,000 at least is needed for repairs and decorations. Donations should be sent to the Rector, Ashwell Rectory.' In 1958, Mrs Wolverley Fordham, outstanding in her service to the village over many years, died suddenly, having just recovered from a broken hip. The Rector's memorial sermon to her memory was a masterpiece of English as well as a beautifully judged tribute. Indeed, as a preacher he was both thought provoking and eloquent.

Looking back at the issues of the Parish or Village News during his ministry, he gives the impression of a man larger than life, bursting with energy, zealously propagating his views but frequently spiced with humour.

As a representative of the Church of England, he had no doubt as to what church everyone should attend. Writing in January 1954 about the Parish Church, he appeals for Christian unity, but very much on his own terms: "It is the mother church of the Parish and well able to supply the worshipping needs for all the people of Ashwell ... How absurd it seems that in a village such as ours there should be religious societies meeting in separate buildings, etc ...". His constant theme is to urge the parishioners of Ashwell to attend the Parish Church.

In August 1967, he again invited all denominations to have their services in the Parish Church. The Roman Catholics were to have their service at 8.00 am and finally finishing at 8.00 pm with a United Service. His appeal fell on deaf ears.

In December 1972 he makes yet another impassioned appeal for all the denominations to worship in the Parish Church. His appeal was ignored.

In November 1969, Jack Catterick invited the Methodists and Congregationalists to join with him in the formation of one Village Sunday School. He was politely refused.

Six months later he put the following in Ashwell News: "To Methodist Members of the Church: As you have only one service on a Sunday at 3.00 pm, the Rector would remind you that communicant members of the Methodist Church are welcome to receive the Sacrament at the Parish Church at any time as equal members".

Jack was a great publicist, fearless propagandist and a bit arrogant in his proclamations and exhortations. In a special sense the Ashwell News was his propaganda weapon. In one issue he writes: "This paper is edited, typed, duplicated and folded by the Rector in between telephone calls, services, callers, meals, etc. He accepts responsibility for all errors!" What a brave man! He would frequently contribute an anonymous article, especially if it was on a provocative subject. He was always proposing something to challenge others, whether in the way they lived their lives, or in the opportunities they had to serve the church.

The church clock

By 1971, Robert Sheldrick had been climbing the 100 steps up to the bellringers' chamber every other day for ten years to laboriously wind up the two heavy weights so that the people of Ashwell would know the time. Before Robert, others had been climbing the steps ever since 1894. Unlike Robert, however, some of them had been paid for their services.

Above Left: *During a gale in 1947 much of the spire leadwork was damaged, the weather cock blown off, and found damaged in Churchmeadow.* (Pictorial/A. W. Sheldrick)

Above Right: *In March 1948, scaffolding was erected, the lead renewed and Fred Bray and Albert Sheldrick replaced the repaired and regilded weather cock on the 176 ft high spire.* (Pictorial/A. W. Sheldrick)

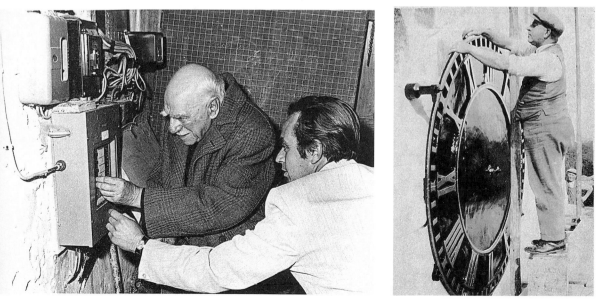

Above Left: *The Church Clock installed in 1896 eventually gave up the ghost. Funds were raised to repair and electrify it, and on November 4th 1971 veteran Church Warden John Sale switched it on, with fund raiser Eric Gurney in attendance.* (Mrs. B. Wallace)

Above Right: *When the Church Tower was restored in the late 1920's Victor Strickland re-gilded the numerals and hands of the clock. The diameter of the clock face is 8 ft, circumference 24 ft 4 ins. The minute hand is 3 ft 10 ins long, the hour hand a bit shorter.* (A. W. Sheldrick)

How the village came by the clock, paid for by a Nonconformist, is told in the following entry in the Ashwell Vestry Book of 3 April 1902.

The church clock

It has been rightly thought that some record expressing a grateful tribute and thanks to the generous donor, and a brief account of its dedication, should find a place in our parish register. The following may be read with interest in the future years. The Church Clock which has three dials, on the East, West and South fronts of the tower, was the gift of the late Joseph Butler Westrope who died at Caldecote, Cambridgeshire, on 13 January 1894 and was interred in Ashwell churchyard on 18 January. By his will he left the sum of £300 for the erection of a chiming clock on Ashwell church tower.

The work was entrusted to and admirably carried out by Messrs Potts & Son of Leeds. A solemn dedication service at its completion was held on 4 November 1896 at 7.00 pm. The church was quite full and an excellent sermon was preached by the Venerable Archdeacon, W J Lawrence of St Albans. During the singing of the Nunc Dimittis the clergy and choir proceeded to the tower.

The Archdeacon read the dedication prayer and the clock was set in motion by the Rector, the Reverend S W P Webb, at exactly one minute to eight. This was done by a string let down from the belfry which, on being pulled, released the pendulum. The chimes after the minute's waiting then played and the clock struck the hour. This was immediately followed by the choir singing beneath the tower "Time is passing, so teach us, O Lord, to number our days that we may apply our hearts with wisdom". [Was this the anthem Panajotti composed specially for the occasion?] After which the clergy and choir returned to their places in the chancel, singing the hymn "O God our help in ages past".

A natural feeling was left behind that as the tower of Ashwell church should stand and the clock go on striking we should not fail to remember the name of the kind donor. It was proposed by Mr W Cooper and seconded by Mr W E Bacon that the foregoing should be entered in the minutes. Carried unanimously."

By the year 1971 the church clock was giving trouble and was in urgent need of a major overhaul and repair. At the same time there was the question as to who was actually responsible for its maintenance. Who had Joey Westrope left it to? Only Joey and Miriam knew, and they were no more. So the Parish Council set up a committee to raise the money for the clock's complete restoration and electrification.

The sum of £1,617 was raised in the village, including a substantial contribution by Mr John Sale in memory of his late wife. He had been present at the age of 17 when the clock was originally started in 1894. The cost of overhauling and electrifying the clock by Messrs Smith of Derby was £1,506, leaving a balance of £111 in the bank.

The ceremony of starting and re-dedicating Ashwell parish church clock was performed on 4 November 1971 at 7.45 pm.

In his address to the Rector, the Chairman of the Parish Council, Geoffrey Coad, said: "Sir, recently, as a result of a village effort, we the people of Ashwell have been able to repair and modernise the clock installed for the benefit of the village in the church tower some 75 years ago. Now, on the completion of the work, we ask you to lead us in the ceremony of re-starting the clock and in a short act of thanksgiving".

The Rector replied: "As guardian of the church and its property, this I will gladly do. With thanksgiving for the loyalty and affection expressed in the work achieved and in the Name of God, Father, Son and Holy Spirit, I dedicate this clock to the welfare and benefit of the people of Ashwell".

After a special hymn, written by the Rector, was sung, John Sale and Robert Sheldrick were invited to start the clock.

After prayers, the Rector, on behalf of the people of Ashwell, presented Robert Sheldrick with two silver candlesticks inscribed 'To Robert Sheldrick, for winding the church clock in Ashwell for many years. 4.11.1971'.

A commemorative plate was affixed to the wall of the tower, which reads: 'The clock was restored in 1971 and re-dedicated on 4 November. The villagers of Ashwell were responsible for the cost in company with John Sale, lately a churchwarden, who made a substantial contribution in memory of his wife'. A bonfire was lit in church meadow to honour the occasion.

In 1993, when for any reason the clock stops, Robert still climbs those 100 steps to re-start it, still giving his services free.

The church tower crisis

When Norman Gurney and his family returned to live in Ashwell in late March, 1975, they held a housewarming party early in May of that year, and quite a few of the party went up the Church Tower. The next day the Tower was put out of bounds.

Headlines in the Press told some of the story: 'Village emergency over church tower threat'. 'Ashwell church tower in danger of collapse'. 'Ashwell church tower situation serious'. 'Church tower plea to PM'. 'MP Mr Ian Stewart to seek state aid for danger tower'. 'District Council discuss church tower'. 'Church repair plea to Council fails'.

'Right to the top'. Churchwarden, Eric Gurney, has gone right to the top to get action. He has written asking for urgent help to the Prime Minister, Harold Wilson, Tony Crosland, Environment Minister, Opposition Leader, Mrs Margaret Thatcher and to Mr Ian Stewart, our MP.

The Government's proposed Bill to give state aid to churches may not become law for eighteen months. "Ashwell church tower cannot wait that long, so we are looking for some government assistance immediately", said Mr Gurney. However, another headline stated, 'Crumbling church is in no danger'.

"A crumbling village church is not a danger to the public" - the verdict of North Herts Council's Planning Officer, Mr Bryan Hull.

Mr Hull said in a report: "The church tower appears to be in a considerable state of disrepair with cracks noticeable on the supporting buttresses facing Mill Street. But my structural advisers could find no apparent evidence of any further deterioration or fallen masonry. I did not deem it necessary to invoke the powers, delegated to me by the committee under the Public Health Acts, from a public safety point of view".

On Friday, 6 June 1975, the Cambridge Evening News reported: 'Danger tower sets a problem. Unless immediate financial help is found, Ashwell's church tower, which is in danger of collapse, may have to be demolished.' On 12 June 1975, Churchwarden Eric Gurney told North Herts District Council Environmental Health Committee that over the last 15 years Ashwell people had spent £15,000 on the church and the tower and the architect, Mr Victor Farrow, said that unless immediate financial help is found the tower, which is in danger of collapse, may have to be demolished. £15,000 was needed for immediate repairs and an appeal Fund was set up. The money was raised and the crumbling buttresses were repaired. But that was only the start.

Nearly £12,500 was raised in 1975 and 1976. Expenditure between 1975 and 1977 on the Tower Restoration was about £14,000.

During the years 1978-1992, nearly £182,000 was spent on the Church Restoration projects, including the Tower. This was funded by an amazing total of just over £217,000, £74,500 coming from grants, £54,000 from various functions and £36,000 from straightforward giving. Over £19,000 came from the General Fund, and nearly £33,000 was earned in interest. High interest rates have their uses! But these staggering figures, even taking inflation into account, tell a remarkable story of fund raising and the funds had £35,000 in hand for future major repairs.

The Church of England, until the great recession of the late 80s and early 90s, was financially buttressed by its investments but by the end of 1992 its losses on these, especially on property investment, had cost about £800,000,000. So whereas in 1939 Ashwell Parish Church contributed £32 to the Diocesan Quota, and in 1975 sent £894, by 1993 it had reached the huge sum of £20,360, basically contributed by its congregation. Where will it end?

A major improvement

About the same time as the church tower was causing great concern, the Parish or Church Room became the subject of considerable controversy. In the 1890s, Rupert Fordham had built the building as a Technical School where evening classes were held to continue the education of Ashwell children who at that time left school at eleven or twelve years of age. It became known as the Technical Room but now is known as the Parish Rooms.

There had been problems as to the ownership of the building. Although Rupert Fordham had wanted to bequeath it to the Diocese of St Albans, he died in 1938 before this could be done. Eventually the Parochial Church Council took steps to establish ownership by statutory declaration, which was obtained in May 1970.

When it became known early in 1975 that the Parochial Church Council was thinking of selling it to the Ashwell Scout Group, the matter was brought up at the Parish Council, involving a disagreement between Geoffrey Coad, then Chairman, and Churchwarden Eric Gurney, who claimed that it was no concern of the Council, while Mr Coad claimed that the Parish Council could discuss anything it wanted to, particularly a matter which was causing much concern to the villagers.

Many were strongly opposed to selling it.

Eventually, after some delay, the sale notice was withdrawn; the Scouts spent over £1,500 on improving the Scout Hut (given years previously by Mrs Wolverley Fordham), near the Village Hall; the Parochial Church Council abandoned plans to build a new hall in the churchyard and prepared plans to modernise and enlarge the building with kitchen and inside toilets.

The Church Room Fund was launched; one benefactor gave £1,000, another offered to pay any interest incurred by borrowing from the Bank to get the job

Left: *H.M. The Queen Mother, with the Rev. J. Catterick and Church Warden Eric Gurney leaving Percy Sheldrick's home after her visit to Ashwell in July 1969.* (Citizen/Anthony Catterick)

Below: *Percy Sheldrick with an outstanding example of his work so much admired by the Queen Mother.* (Museum)

Some of the volunteers who worked on the renovation of the Parish Room in the mid-70's. L-R: David Dixon, John Smith, Liz Godsman, (later Gurney) Alan White, Anthony Catterick, Audrey Gurney, Eric Gurney on the tractor. Stuart Gurney and Peter Moore. (Eric Gurney)

done. Others gave generously or ran activities to raise money. The Department of Education provided a substantial grant. Much of the work was done by a team of about 12 volunteers, aged from 10-70. The job was completed early in 1976 and the Parish Rooms were opened for Sunday teas and meetings of all kinds.

Royal Visitors and a Politician

During Jack Catterick's ministry Ashwell had two royal visitors and the man who nearly became Prime Minister, Rt Hon R A Butler, later Lord Butler. On 21 October 1959 the Evening Standard carried the following article:

> Today is Mr Butler's wedding day. He and Mrs Mollie Courtauld are being married at the Church of St Mary the Virgin, Ashwell, near Baldock, Herts. The ceremony will be performed by the Bishop of Chelmsford, the Rt Rev Falkner Allison, assisted by the Rector of Ashwell, the Rev John Catterick. It will be a family wedding, with only 30 members from each of the two families. Ashwell, quite inured to the unusual by now, will see nothing strange in a "Secret Wedding" with 60 persons, and a considerable body of Press at the ancient lych gate.
>
> Mr Butler drives from his home at Halstead to arrive at the church a few minutes before Mrs Courtauld, who will travel from Great Yeldham.
>
> The bride and groom intend to spend a few days abroad, and return for the opening of Parliament next Tuesday.'

Although the wedding plans had been kept secret, Mr R A Butler and Mrs Courtauld, whose daughter, Perina Fordham, at that time lived locally, had been seen in and around Ashwell.

Ashwell had to wait until July 1969 before receiving a royal personage, and then the visit was so secret that only a handful of people saw Queen Elizabeth, the Queen Mother. The rest didn't know, until they read about it on the following Friday in the local press.

The Queen Mother was spending the weekend at St Paul's Walden Bury when Lady Bowes-Lyon suggested a visit to Ashwell. A telephone call was made on the Saturday, asking the Rector, Jack Catterick, to arrange for a private visit on the following day to the church and museum, with no publicity, red carpet or police. The Queen Mother, accompanied by Lady Bowes-Lyon, Lady Radnor and Mr Thomas Gough, arrived at the church at 2.30 pm where they were met by the Rector and Mrs Judy Catterick, Church lay reader, Mr John Smith and Mrs Smith, Mr Guy Barrett, head server, Mr Eric Gurney, Churchwarden, with his three children, Linda, Stuart and Heather; Mr Peter Rose, organist, and Mr Clive Whitby, the Verger, who acts as guide to the many visitors to the church.

As the party was shown around the church (Peter Rose quietly playing the Snetzler chamber organ, on loan from Thurston Dart), the Queen Mother was especially interested in a tapestry, 'Christ in Glory', which was the work of Percy Sheldrick, Albert Sheldrick's uncle, and asked if she could visit him to see more of his work.

Eric Gurney went along to give Percy advance warning and he said, "The Lord told me something special was going to happen today", and asked Eric to give him time to tidy up before she arrived! Before leaving the church, her Majesty spoke to three children from the Nobel Grammar School and the Camps Hill Junior School, Stevenage, who were working on a school project dealing with the Black Death. Then, after signing the church visitors' book, the Royal party walked over to the Museum. The Rector introduced Albert Sheldrick, curator and author, to the Queen Mother, who then spent twenty minutes showing knowledge of antiquities and her great interest in the collection.

After another book signing, these distinguished visitors, after being quickly snapped by Mrs Crump's camera, joined the two cars on their way to view Percy's tapestries.

It has been leaked (not on tape!) that the Queen Mother has lunch from time to time with her trainer at The Jester Hotel, not far from the one time Duke of Devonshire's Odsey Race Course.

Just over a year later, the Cottage Garden Fund Committee sent a request to the Queen Mother for a contribution, which she graciously gave. Incidentally, Lord Butler, referred to earlier, also sent a generous donation.

The following account appeared in the local newspaper, The Citizen, on 24 December, 1971: 'Special preparations are customary when royalty drops in, and the scene at Ashwell church on Monday was no exception to that rule - even though the visiting monarch was Henry the Eighth with one of his six wives! At 8.30 am, a convoy of cars, caravans, coaches and lorries parked in the lane outside the churchyard and a small army of over 140 actors, extras and production crew members from the Elstree film studios at Borehamwood, captained by director, Waris Hussein, converged upon the 600-year-old church.

Frances Cuka, playing Catherine of Aragon, sat in full costume with a leather handbag on her knee, patiently waiting for the transformation of the church to be completed, and her "king", Keith Michell, so successful in the BBC series, to finish his own preparation in a private caravan.

Sightseers looked on from the back, and small boys asked the extras for their autographs. Someone announced: "I think we should avoid smoking in church", and cigarettes were scrupulously left burning in niches in the thick outside walls as their owners looked in to see how much longer they had to wait.

Finally the church was ready for the first of the two scenes to be shot: Henry, bearded and slim during his marriage to Catherine of Aragon, visiting an abbey with her to touch a holy relic and pray for a male heir.

By the time the second scene was shot darkness had fallen and eerily the actors re-enacted history as they looted the "abbey" after the dissolution of the monasteries. A similar fate had befallen Ashwell church at the same time.

Jack Catterick's crowning achievement
The Ashwell Festival

The Ashwell Festival started almost by accident. Jack Catterick, himself a talented musician, had a very musical wife, a pianist who became an organist for Ashwell's church services, and four sons, choristers at All Saints, Margaret Street in London, Westminster Abbey and King's College, Cambridge. The boys, together with another musical friend, Jeremy Symonds, planned a singing holiday at Blakeney on the north Norfolk coast but, as this proved too difficult to organise, the group gathered at Ashwell instead.

In the early years, boys and men came from Cathedrals and Choir Schools all over the country - Cambridge, Oxford, Worcester, Peterborough, Derby, Guildford, Southwell, Lichfield, Hampstead Parish Church and many more. Well-known people from the arts world, including Thurston Dart, Sir David Willcocks, Alan Ridout, Herbert Howells, Margaret Cable, Brian Judge, Norman Shelley, Patric Dickinson, James Blades, Henry Sandon, John Russell and Philip Moore, The Elizabethans, came to Ashwell for the first two weeks in August to sing in the great 14th century church, in local halls or in the marquee on the Rectory lawn. The original patrons were: The Bishop of St Albans, Sir William McKie, Professor Patrick Hadley and Elizabeth Poston.

Choristers slept on the Rectory dining room floor, in garages and various barns converted to dormitories. A system evolved whereby Ashwell villagers offered bed and breakfast to the visitors and the School cook, Mrs Violet Crack (known to the choristers as 'Auntie Vi'), together with volunteers from the Ashwell Church Choir and the parish, performed culinary miracles, providing three meals a day for 40-50 performers in the Church Room. Rehearsals were held in the mornings, with the afternoons free for sports or outings. Services, recitals and concerts were held every evening. John Russell, one of the early Directors of Music, broadcast on the BBC European Service on 2 September, 1960 about the Festival. It describes Ashwell as well as the Festival, as only a stranger can.

"The first thing you notice about the village of Ashwell is that you can stroll down its streets without having to jump out of the way of traffic. For Ashwell is on the road to nowhere, and the sudden sense of leisure and freedom is made all the more vivid by the fact that the village is only five miles from Britain's main arterial road, the A1. You fight your way out of London and are caught up in the rat-race of England's heaviest traffic as far as Baldock in Hertfordshire; and there you turn off to the right and wander over gentle hills, through open corn-land, without walls or hedges, and with only a few trees. It all looks rather continental, and perhaps it is that which already casts a slight enchantment over the traveller at this point, so that he reaches the summit of the last rise expecting to see what he does see - a wooded hollow, with apparently no road leading out of it, a cluster of houses and, in the middle of it all, a huge thirteenth century church, so vast, and with a steeple so high, that at first it seems to assault the eye with a kind of visual explosion. Down the last hill, and we are in Ashwell. The lanes are narrow; the little shops are typical village shops; the houses are typical cottages, giving directly on to the street, with their gardens at the back. The sun shines, the birds sing. It would all be a simple picturesque corner of rural England, were it not for that towering cliff of a church, commanding the attention, seen all the time out of the corner of the eye. We must dispose of it; come to terms with it. We walk round it, a little warily, and call at the Rectory to search out the incumbent. He will surely be a mild ageing country parson, traditional and comfortable. He will soon remove the drama from this forbidding semi-cathedral of his. He will wander round it with us, talking in mellow tones of the parsons who came before him, the crops, some unusual tracings near the west window, and we will take it all for granted. We knock at the yellow Rectory door and we meet the Rector of Ashwell, the Reverend Jack Catterick.

"Alas for our hopes. The impact of its Rector is not a whit less violent than that of the church. He is a dynamo, and the Rectory is a power house. We soon discover that. The great church is not to him merely a convenient and appropriate building in which to hold the regulation Church of England services; it is a centre of all spiritual activities which are conducted to the greater glory of God, and these of course include pictorial art and music. The village is not to him a peaceful collection of cottages housing a community of fair-weather Christians, but a row of citadels to be stormed by the might of the Creator in whom Jack Catterick believes so simply and so whole-heartedly.

"For the last seven years he has given expression to his convictions by holding a Festival of Music and Art in the Church, and that is where I myself came in. As a professional musician, knowing nothing of the village or its Rector or, indeed, very much about church music, my first knock on the yellow door three years ago has certainly reverberated ever since. For I seem to have become Director of Music of the Ashwell Festival, and the ten days of music-making in that great church have been the high spot in my busy year. Just as he drew me in, so he draws in the singing men and boys from the Cathedrals of Peterborough, Ely, Derby, Southwell, to join with the nucleus of his village choir to form a Festival chorus. The village people find beds for some of them in their homes and help with the cooking; others live a cheery barrack-room life in converted Rectory outhouses or tents. We all meet for meals in the Parish Room, whose apparently limitless hospitality extends to the BBC engineers and the composers of new festival music. The Rector's wife, Eileen, watches over it all with an unruffled charm. The days are crowded, noisy and very happy. The mornings are taken up with intensive rehearsals, the afternoons are officially free, so that the choirboys can get up to holiday mischief before singing like little angels in the evening; there is rehearsal again at 5.30 and the performance at 8.00. Then, after a late snack in the Refectory, the pattern becomes a little confused. The Festival seems to develop two storm-centres, so to speak. One of them settles in the Rectory drawing room, where the Rector's eldest son of 21 and my own eldest of 18 bring out their guitars and beat up a skiffle session among the adolescents of the neighbourhood. The other invades the Saloon Bar of the Bushel and Strike, a glorious pub, otherwise known as the 'Thirst after Righteousness'. Here anything can happen, from impromptu Tudor madrigals to outrageous gossip about musical personalities and a swapping of the latest robust story. After closing time, the two groups merge in the Rectory, often to listen to a recording of the evening's performance or to sing round the piano. It is all very noisy and relaxing.

"But it is the last Evensong which sums up. The vast church is full; not only of people, but of village garden flowers and examples of pictorial art from great names and small. The Festival Choir, fully robed, is giving the first liturgical performance of a service which has been written in the new musical language. It was composed especially by a young musician, Alan Ridout, already making his name in secular music. It includes - naturally for Ashwell - many opportunities for the congregation to take part in the service. Music and Art, Parish and People, the ancient and the modern, are joined together to the greater glory of God. The great church is still powerful but no longer intimidating.

So - if you should ever find yourselves knocking upon Ashwell Rectory's yellow door - beware! You'll be back, doing something, either frying sausages or singing Palestrina, or devising some method of getting the choirboys to bed at a reasonable hour.

"But you'll be back!"

In its earlier years, the Festival spanned a fortnight in August and on once occasion the boys wanted a cricket match. Jack Catterick approached the Village Cricket club and as a result a match was played on the Recreation Ground for the first time on a Sunday.

Soon afterwards, the Club Fixtures began to include Sunday matches which the Rector was willing to tolerate if the players would attend a specially arranged late evensong. According to Byron Searle, the cricketers kept their side of the bargain but the Rector's own 'thirst after righteousness' made him give up the late service before the sportsmen! But to return to the Festival. The Parish Church choir, stimulated to high standards by the impact of all this high quality music, improved out of all recognition and in August, 1970, the Festival was re-named "Ashwell Church Week", with the Church choir taking a leading role, instead of visiting choristers. Three years earlier, Eileen Catterick had died of a heart attack at the age of 60 and the following year Judith Brown married the Rector. Both his

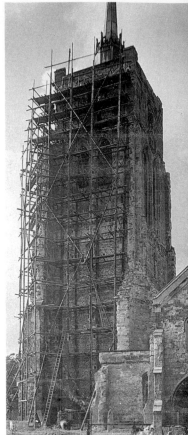

Above: *The Church Tower surrounded by scaffolding in the 1928 restoration– a most interesting picture.* (A. Sheldrick)

Left: *The T.V. camera's filmed the service which was seen on Anglia Television on Sunday 30th August 1962.* (Anthony Catterick)

Ashwell's Music Festival started in 1953 with visiting choristers from various Choir Schools. This is the 1955 choir.
(Anthony Catterick)

The choir, mostly Ashwellians, which sang in the Festival in 1970, called Ashwell Church Week.
Back Row: Guy Barrett, Martin Sheard, Michael Smedley, Willie Scott, Terry Hatchett, Martin
Geeves, John Anderson, Rodney Worboys, Nigel Bishop, David Ward.
Centre: Judith Hayes, Judy Catterick, Linda Gurney, Ann Anderson, Jan Fletcher, Marion
Worboys, Pamela Harrison, Audrey Gurney.
Front: Jayne Coote, Olive Anderson, Julie Braithwaite, Patsy Duffy, Sarah Bishop, Francis Coad,
Katharine Stemp. N.B. The ladies have new robes made by Audrey Gurney.
(Herts Pictorial/Anthony Catterick)

Ashwell Parish Church Choir, 1975. Back l to r: *Ken Rook, Jeremy Symonds , Rodney*
Worboys, Peter Rose, Stuart Gurney, Francis Coad, Heather Gurney, Ian Ray (organist) Andrew
Pearson, Teresa Bishop, Tony Gee, Martin Sheard, Terry Hatchett. Front: *Gareth Harris, Lucy*
Coad, Linda Gee, Marion Worboys, Judy Catterick, Olive Anderson, Claire Gurney, Glenys Travis
(Olive Anderson)

wives were dedicated to supporting Jack's musical ventures, and in 1994 Judy will have completed thirty years as Director of Music of Ashwell Church Choir.

Thereafter, the basic pattern of the Festival revolved around the Parish Church Choir, still happily augmented by visiting musicians and during the Festival directed and accompanied by top class professionals. Under Jack's successor, the Reverend John Mullett, the time of the Festival changed from a week in August to one in late April/early May.

In 1993, the Festival celebrated its 40th anniversary and its programme was quite typical of its predecessors. The Ashwell Theatre Club presented 'The Hollow Crown', in which Jeremy Symonds, one of the founders of the Festival, took part; some young Cambridge University musicians gave a concert; there was a performance by the Norwich Puppet Theatre and an evening of opera sung by students from the National Opera Studio.

The climax of the week was a Sung Eucharist in which the Ashwell Choir was joined by the Pro Musica Singers from Oxford, conducted by Michael Smedley, who had attended the Festival in its early years as a chorister from Southwell Minster. (The Pro Musica had been finalists in the BBC's Choir of the Year Competition in 1992.) The organist was Paul Bryan, Director of Music at St John's College Choir School in Cambridge. The Celebrant and Preacher was Archbishop Lord Runcie, previously Archbishop of Canterbury and a former Bishop in the St Albans Diocese. A crowded church, some unforgettable music, joyous reunions with former Festival participants, including those of two of Jack's sons - Michael and Anthony, (Peter had died of a heart attack in 1989 and Christopher was unable to attend) - and an Archbishop's sermon - these were a tribute to the enduring work of Jack Catterick.

His ministry at Ashwell ended in 1977, forced upon him by ill health.

But in the 1976 January issue Village News he writes in a way which epitomises the man and his mission:

What a beautiful Christmas it was
I have just spent a few minutes looking back over the Festival. There was the excellent Senior Citizen's Party on 13 December and then on the following Monday the Children's Christmas Service, as usual beautifully done and bringing a splendid collection of toys for the poor children of Battersea. Later in the week there was the children's Christmas Dinner where Teachers and Governors became waiters, though later to enjoy a splendid meal provided by Mrs Ball and her helpers. (Did anyone ever present a better and more succulent steak than the one I enjoyed?) And back to the Church - on the Sunday before Christmas another play presented by members of Children's Special. And almost before we knew it Christmas Eve with the church beautifully decorated after being mop-washed by Clive. At 7.30 pm it all became alive when for the first time for months the bells pealed out - what a delightful surprise, devised by Robert Sheldrick. Then the midnight mass, the packed church, half lit, the chancel sparkling with candles like a starlit sky, and for the first time since May the organ, or that part of it which has been reassembled, pealed out the angels' song. On Christmas Morning again the Church was packed for the village service - a joyful occasion full of fun and worship.

But for me perhaps the greatest occasion was the next day taking the Sacrament to some of those unable to attend a service - the old and sick. All was quiet, not a soul about and one walked alone with God.

In 1979 he returned with Judy to his beloved Ashwell and that beautiful voice was stilled in May 1983.

Ashwell at Leisure

After World War Two, when so many leisure activities had had to be abandoned, the Parish Council spent a great deal of time deliberating on the state of the Recreation Ground, a fine village amenity, which needed, however, constant attention. Keeping the grass cut, areas of scrub tidied and the tall elm trees surrounding it lopped and made safe were always on the agenda. Even in the 1950s, vandals were active in damaging the seats round the edge of the ground; the children's playground equipment was frequently damaged and constantly in need of repair. Complaints that the (so called) toilets behind the old Pavilion - merely a narrow passage shielded from the adjoining land by a corrugated iron fence, with no roof and no drains - were disgustingly dirty, especially after the Feast, were frequent.

Neither the Football nor the Cricket Club were very satisfied with the amenities.

The old pavilion - built in the early years of this century when the grass was kept short by grazing sheep and made of timber with a galvanised iron roof - needed a great deal of repair in 1947. But Charles Westrope got a team together and repaired the building at no cost to the Council.

A new pavilion

From time to time, the possibility of a new Pavilion was raised. In 1934, the Cricket Club had started a fund for one and the Jubilee of King George V in 1935 and the Coronation of King George VI in 1937 raised £75. The war intervened and curtailed all such activities, but the matter began to be seriously discussed in 1952 with the forthcoming Coronation of Queen Elizabeth when it was realised that a fund existed. The celebrations of the Coronation took the form of a Sports Day which was highly successful and this annual event has continued ever since. £80 was added to the Pavilion Fund and, by 1955, the Fund stood at over £300.

As with many village activities there were many problems and setbacks. In 1956 the Sports Day Committee resigned - so much effort but so little profit was their complaint. A special Pavilion Committee, however, was set up under Bill Reeves' Chairmanship and various fund raising ventures were proposed, some of which were successful and others met with little response. In April 1957 an artist's impression of the Pavilion was on display, designed by architect, Winton Aldridge and again in January 1958 the Committee was on the point of resigning, their grouses having to be aired at a Special Meeting with the Parish Council.

Much of that year was spent in arguing about where exactly the Pavilion should be sited. By now it was clear that substantial grants would be available from the County Council and Department of Education and in 1959 building work commenced. Joe Capon and Albert Sheldrick were asked by Bill Reeves to get together a band of volunteers. The foundations were laid and after a prefabricated sectional timber building was erected, these volunteers got to

Above: Displays by The Veteran Car Club of Great Britain, held in mid-August in Elbrook Meadow from 1958, now a regular part of the August Bank Holiday Show. (Lindsay Colquhoun)

Below: *Sports Day in June 1973 on the Rec.* (Linday Colquhoun)

work. As the Opening Ceremony Programme states: "Drainage, water supply and all fittings, electric wiring and fittings, internal decoration, outside paving - all these problems had to be faced. As with the foundations, voluntary labour completed all these tasks without a single groan. No words could adequately convey the thanks of the community to the volunteers".

It was a splendid effort, splendidly tackled by young and old. The Pavilion, opened on Whit Monday, 6 June, 1960, just over a quarter of a century after its erection had been proposed, has been a great benefit to the village and visiting sports enthusiasts.

To pee or not to pee (with apologies to Shakespeare!)

One achievement completed leads on to the next, and for some years the need for a Public Convenience in Ashwell had been discussed by the Parish Council, way back in 1949. Plans for one were part of an ambitious scheme to improve the Recreation Ground, which actually never got off, let alone on, the ground! The matter of a WC was discussed off and on for another 10 years, and in March 1959 the Rural District Council gave permission to the Parish Council to build its own toilets. But this was regarded as a thinly disguised attempt to escape from its own responsibilities and the Annual Parish Meeting emphatically repudiated the idea.

The new pavilion did have toilet facilities and at the Parish Meeting of 1961 it was suggested these could be adapted for public use. However, John Bray pointed out that the Parish Council had no power or funds to maintain WCs. Eventually, in 1970, the RDC agreed that they should be provided and, in January 1971, to be built on the site of the old Telephone Exchange in Alms Lane - an idea which was soon flushed away.

The new Pavilion was in need of improvements and eventually it was agreed to modify the building so that WCs could be added at either end. By September 1974, the work was completed.

There is no record of an Opening Ceremony.

Nearly twenty years later, unlike so many public conveniences elsewhere, they remain open until early evening, kept clean and tidy under the eagle eye of Fred Bryant.

Ashwell's senior citizens' club (AS)

A special Parish meeting was held at the Congregational Church hall in January 1952 to consider setting up an Old People's Welfare Committee and an Over Sixties Club. Nine years later, at the Annual Parish Meeting, schoolmaster Tom Pryor suggested that it formed an Over Sixties Club which could use the Pavilion, when it was built. But it was not until the 1968 Annual Parish Meeting that Frank Gentle was able to announce a Senior Citizens' Club had been formed and was meeting weekly at the Congregational Church hall. This was nearly twenty years after the original suggestion for an Over Sixties Club had come from the members of the Congregational Church. The first general meeting of the club was held at St George's Hall, in the Bushel & Strike, in October 1967, when

The first Annual Dinner of the Senior Citizens Club, December 1967.

(The Royston Crow / May Cook)

The Senior Citizens won the Finch Memorial Rosebowl beating all comers at crib, whist and dominoes in the Herts Age Concern Games Competition. Standing l to r: Fred Brown, Ada Hale, Reg Chaffey, Gladys Izzard, Reg Duffy. Seated: Lou Skerman, Lil Waldock, Joe Capon, Mrs. Westerman, Milly Gallant (May Cook)

The Engine Flower Show, 1950's. L to R: R. Rowlands, C. Bonnett, G. Berry, O. Reynolds, Mrs. Leeke, D. Leeke, D. Bryant, Mrs. A. Covington, Mr. Chapman (Judge), A. Covington (Landlord). (Roy Bonnett)

The Rose and Crown Harvest Festival, 1950's. L to R: L. Bryant, A. Brown, W. Pidgeon, C. Clements, Rev. J. Catterick. Celebrations continued after closing time, but when our local policeman visited the Pub with his new Superintendent, possibly hoping for a spectacular headline – local Rector caught drinking after hours – all were devoutly bowing their heads in prayer!

(Anthony Catterick)

40 people attended and appointed George Berry as Chairman, Harry Finch, Landlord of the Bushel & Strike, as Honorary Treasurer, John Smith as Honorary Secretary and Bill Stimson as Assistant Secretary. The Committee consisted of Mr & Mrs R Jarman, Mrs C Wilkins, Mrs T Mitchell, Mrs V Barton, Mr F Gentle, Mr F Hardiman, Mr C Haylock and Mrs A Chamberlain.

A meeting of the committee was held a few days later when the Chairman stated that a Christmas dinner was being planned. There would be some entertainment and Howard Day had promised a cake. It was agreed that men, 65 and over, and ladies, 60 and over, should be eligible for membership which should be for residents of the village, and that the annual subscription should be 2/6d. Anyone unable to afford this would not, however, be excluded from the club.

The first Christmas Dinner was a great success. 144 chicken portions were ordered, members supplied milk, bread, potatoes, etc and a good time was had by all.

In 1968, the club made its headquarters at the Congregational Church hall, having agreed a weekly rent of 10/-. The opening ceremony on 20 February was performed by the Chairman of the Herts Old People's Welfare Council.

From then on the club was a great success, with coffee evenings, a Derby sweep, Bingo, Bring & Buy evenings, a Harvest Festival in September, the service taken by Fred Sillence, the Congregational Church Pastor. A Thrift Club, Christmas Shopping outings, Slide Shows, Coach Outings and Mystery Tours were also organised.

Today, with new people at the helm, the Ashwell Senior Citizens' Club flourishes, due to the hard work back in 1967 of George Berry and the Committee, not forgetting Frank Gentle, who drove his coach round the village to pick up members and return them safely after closing time.

Most Tuesday evenings, Dave Seaby, my near neighbour in Letchworth, takes his Mother, who is now in her nineties, over to the club where she enjoys a natter with that sadly diminishing number of her old Ashwell friends.

Sport

A lot of water has bubbled out of the Springs since Ashwell's archers hurried down Butt Way to practise on the butts in Bennett's Lane, or even since the crowds were entertained at the cock fights or kicking matches in the meadow behind Ashwell Surgery in Gardiners Lane.

Ashwell had a men's Hockey Team in the First World War and Football and Cricket flourished, encouraged by Headmasters Morgan Biles and his successor, Geoffrey Whitby.

Before we had a Recreation Ground, football was played on Football Close, which was part of the Bury Meadow. In the 1920s, cup ties and important matches were played on the field where Sam Wallace grows strawberries because the ground at that time was enclosed and spectators could be charged for admission.

When the Recreation Ground was provided, the Football Club was one of its first users.

During the Second World War, soldiers from the Bygrave Army Camp obtained permission to play football on the 'Rec'. The village side did not function because so many of its best players were in the Army. But after the war, it had a strong team, and on Easter Monday in 1947 it narrowly lost 5:4 to Knebworth in the Greg Cup Final, which was played on Hitchin Town's Ground. We had some revenge three days later, beating Knebworth 3:1 on the old Stevenage Town ground, which is now where the Station has been built.

We eventually won the Greg Cup in 1961. The Cricket and Football clubs shared the old Pavilion, now used to store sports equipment, and visiting Football Teams had to change in the Rose and Crown in the room which is now its restaurant. Both clubs had provided a lot of free labour to dig the footings, laid the base and dug trenches for the new Pavilion.

Harris's Fair was a regular feature - visiting Ashwell on the Anniversary of the Ashwell Feast, the first Monday and Tuesday after the first Sunday in July. Byron Searle writes: "The early years after the war we always looked out for the steam engines pulling the trailers onto the Rec with the Dodgems, Galloping Horses, Swinging Boats, Cakewalk, etc - quite an event in those days".

In 1981, the Football Club folded. Byron had been its Secretary for thirteen years, up to 1979 and new leaders were not forthcoming. Happily, some of Ashwell's young men, have had the initiative to start it again in 1992, with District Councillor Andrew Young as Manager.

The Cricket Club re-started in 1946 with only one team, whereas before the war Ashwell had two with full fixture lists.

The old Pavilion, which could be opened up with three shutters to watch the match, was where the team changed; tea was served to the players at The Cricketers' Pub, until it closed down in 1959. The new Pavilion came just in time. Cricket was only played on a Saturday, Whit Monday, the Monday of Ashwell Feast and August Bank Holiday Monday.

Cricket was never played on a Sunday until 1955 when the visiting choristers for the Festival played the village team with the ecclesiastical blessing of Rector, Jack Catterick. And from 1956, Sunday fixtures were a regular feature.

Ashwell's Cricket Club played competitive cricket for the Millman Trophy, being a founder member in 1971. So far we haven't won it, but have been Runners Up. We play about twenty friendlies, and enter 5 knockout evening competitions, having won the Royston Keatley Cup three times and been Runners Up several times.

Other sports have flourished. In the 1930s there were Tennis Courts on the Rec at the eastern end, but these fell into disuse after the Second World War and in spite of some ambitious plans for various sports on the Rec, these never came to anything. The Tennis Courts in the grounds of the Further Education Centre have for many years been used by the Tennis Club. The children's playground in one corner of the Rec was a constant cause of concern to the Parish Council, the equipment inadequate and frequently needing repair, often due to vandalism even in the 50s and 60s. At least in the 90s, the play area and equipment are in a good state.

In the 50s and 60s there was a Bowls Club on the land of its then owners, the Williamson family in Green Lane, and Badminton has been played in the Barn next to Zoar Chapel in Gardiners Lane since the 1920s.

Left: *The "Old Merchant Taylor's" Football team 1946-47. Back row L to R: Fred Gallop, Harold Waldock, Jim Davis, 'Bunny' Dellar, Ted Eversden, Arthur Waldock. Front row: Albert Chandler, Sid Waldock, Sid Cheetham, Jack Oyston, Percy Pettengell.* (Nancy Eversden)

Right: *The team of 1953-54. Back row: F. Bryant, R. Skerman, R. Mitchell, E. Eversden, G. Picking, G. Gallant. Front row: J. Dellar, R. Davis, P. Hankin, D. Moule, A. Chandler.* (Marjorie Gentle)

Greg Cup Winners in the 1961-62 season after two replays. Back row l to r: Albert Chandler, I. Savage, Bob Neaves, Taffy Hall, Ken Knock, Roger Dilley, Peter Bryant, Theo Worboys. Front row: Peter Hankin, Richard Andrews, Maurice Skinner, Neil Manly, Rodney Worboys. Mascot Stuart Skerman. (Herts Pictorial/Museum)

The Rose and Crown Darts Outing July 1952. Back row L to R: W. Law, W. Gentle, J. Waldock,
B. Gentle, Noah Geeves, Not Known, B. Worboys, S. Collins, E. Worboys, S. Sheldrick,
H. Sheldrick, R. Gifford, W. Worboys, P. James. Middle row: H. Warboys, N. Moule, B. Dellar,
G. Chapman, A. Waldock, B. Carter. Seated: R. G. Currell, J. Skerman, V. Eley, G. Brown,
G. Collins, T. Eley. (Marjorie Gentle)

Another Rose and Crown outing by Blue Cream Coaches, 1950's. Back row l to r: N. Geeves,
E. Worboys, S. Gentle, B. Worboys, ?. Hoy, H. Worboys, R. Davis, ? Brown, S. Collins, W. Law,
C. Bonnett, S. Waldock, J. Waldock, ? Chamberlain, Unknown, C. Westerman, Unknown,
W. Pidgeon, J. Chaffey, G. Moule, G. Chapman. Front: A. Eley, G. Worboys, A. Waldock,
P. Hankin, A. Brown, G. Collins, T, Turner, B. Dellar, B. Carter. (Roy Bonnett)

Mrs Phyllis Fordham crowns the May Queen 1940-41. The older girls were evacuees. The younger ones on the platform were Bessie Wallace's daughters – Margaret Wallace, Catherine Westrope and Wendy Moynihan. The three in front were Mary Oyston, Judith Hancock and Janet Northern. (Mrs B. Wallace)

In memory of 21 happy years of guiding in Hertfordshire 1919 – 1940 Phyllis Fordham

Above: *Workers at the Fordham Brewery.*
L to R: *Ben Seaby, Alf Ketteridge, Herbert Pack, "Snowy" Reynolds, Jack Davis.* (Mrs. L. MacBeth)

Left: *This must have been a great occasion for Phyllis Fordham when the then Queen attended this Hertfordshire Guides Rally.* (Gurney Sheppard)

The uniformed organisations - Brownies, Guides, Cubs and Scouts, flourished both during the Second World War and afterwards. Mrs Wolverley Fordham was a prominent leader of the Guides, not just in Ashwell, and would be saddened to know that in 1990 the Guides were disbanded because there was no one willing to lead them.

The Scouts continue to occupy the single storey building just outside the Village Hall, and constantly spend money, time and effort to keep it habitable.

During the 1950s, a great deal of emphasis was laid on providing facilities for youth and this has helped to keep the Youth Club going, now under the voluntary leadership of Robert Chandler.

Sports Day on Whit Monday has been a regular part of Ashwell's sporting activities for many years, although it had a bit of a bumpy start.

Ashwell Men's Club, formed in 1922, the original venue being the Old Maltings Building next to the Village Hall, was open all weekday evenings except Thursdays.

It was very popular, and even put on a pantomime, 'Cinderella', with an all male cast in 1934.

It started a Christmas Fund in 1941 for members serving in the Forces. The Club organised a Billiards and Snooker Exhibition in 1957 which raised £60, enough then to train a Guide Dog for the Blind. In the 50s, other attractions and the lack of new blood made Alan Picking and the Committee decide to close it in 1962.

Although there was no Horticultural Society in Ashwell, and with the new style of the post-war Ashwell Show, the Flower and Vegetable Show had no part in it, the Engine Pub in 1950 became the venue for a similar show on the last Saturday in August. This was also in aid of the blind, the fund being called 'The Engine Aid the Blind Fund'. All the produce had to be sold for the Fund, after judging. Landlord, Albert Covington, and George Berry were two of the leading lights of this Show, which went on for nearly ten years, but ended when the latter fell ill.

Ashwell's Bank Holiday Show (NJG)

When did it start? The 1987 Programme states - 'We are celebrating the Diamond celebration of Ashwell Show - although this in itself could be in dispute'. It is certainly true that in 1927, the Rector, Rev Henry Griffith, wrote in the Parish Magazine: "I believe the revival of the Ashwell Flower Show will be very welcome". The Parochial Church Council had been authorised to promote a Fete and Flower Show on August Bank Holiday then and until 1966, held on the first Monday in August. It has been suggested that the first Show was in 1921 but I came across a Show programme for 1890 entitled 'Ashwell and District Flower Show and Athletic Sports' which, while quite different from modern Shows, was clearly a forerunner of them. Before 1939, it was mainly a Fete, Flower and Vegetable Show plus all sorts of entertainments. As John Beresford described it in 1932: "... as the village is large, we can carry off, with dignity and ease, pony and horse gymkhanas, a Flower Show, a poultry and whatnot Show (this included rabbits and canaries, etc) and variety entertainment provided ... by first class companies of London artistes. Among the latter, the prime piece is that of 'The Strongest Boy in the World'".

The first Show after the Second World War was in 1948 - when it was very much a Horse Show and Gymkhana. It was in aid of the Spire Restoration Fund, as the Spire had been badly damaged the year before and the weathercock blown off. On the Horse Show side, Kathleen Angell, now Mrs Mack, was the guiding spirit and insisted on everything being of the highest quality including the Rosettes. With the 1949 Show, £2,000 had been raised, more than enough to achieve the needs of the Restoration Fund. Then in 1952 there was no Show but Albert Bush and Mrs Fordham worked hard and successfully to revive it in 1953.

Albert was a newcomer to Ashwell in 1946. Demobbed from the War, working in London, finding it difficult to obtain accommodation for his wife and two children, Albert worked in the same office as Courtney Patten, whose father was a Director of the Tea Wholesalers in Jessamine House. Through Courtney, Albert learned of a cottage available from Whitby Farm. When interviewed by old Mrs Angell, she said that if he was a farm worker his rent would be 2/6d a week: as he wasn't, 7/6d. They moved into the cottage - 2 Partridge Hill. It had an outside toilet, no electricity, and no water. Although there was a 40 foot well, the water was polluted. So every day Albert's wife, Edna, had to collect buckets of water from Partridge Hall! Their first winter was the horrific one of 1947. Albert was one of Ashwell's first commuters, catching the steam train from Stevenage. The journey from and to Ashwell took two and a half hours each way! In 1950 the family moved to Dixies Close, and it was here in his front room, the Ashwell Show was saved by a meeting of interested persons, urged on by the Parish Council, who decided that it should be carried on, after it failed to take place in 1952.

From then on, the Show has been held in unbroken succession, although in many ways its character, extent and profitability to the village have changed enormously.

From 1968 to 1976, the Show made an average yearly profit of nearly £800.

In 1992, the profits were £11,000 and in 1993 attendance reached an all time high, exceeding 16,000 people.

With a remarkable range of events and activities, the presence of 85 Trade Stands, first introduced in 1982, with a dedicated Committee headed by Dr Martin Hoffman, its future seems assured.

And Albert, the man who saved the Show, has also played important roles connected with the Village Hall and the Horticultural society, proving that commuters can be a great blessing.

Ashwell Theatricals (Pauline Whitby)

Theatrical activity in Ashwell goes back a long way. The earliest plays on record were performed by members of the Women's Institute and produced by Mrs. Gladys Raikes of Ducklake Farm, who was an expert and meticulous producer. The first one was *Square Pegs*, by Lawrence Houseman, which was performed in the Bury Gardens. Later productions included a Nativity play in the church, and

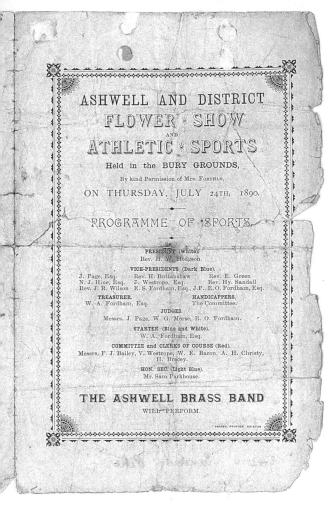

ASHWELL AND DISTRICT
FLOWER · SHOW
AND
ATHLETIC · SPORTS

Held in the BURY GROUNDS,

By kind Permission of Mrs. FORDHAM,

ON THURSDAY, JULY 24TH, 1890.

PROGRAMME OF SPORTS

PRESIDENT (White).
Rev. H. W. Hodgson.

VICE-PRESIDENTS (Dark Blue).
J. Page, Esq.   Rev. H. Buttanshaw   Rev. E. Green
N. J. Hine, Esq.   J. Westrope, Esq.   Rev. Hy. Sandall
Rev. J. R. Wilson   E. S. Fordham, Esq., J.P. E. O. Fordham, Esq.

TREASURER.   HANDICAPPERS.
W. A. Fordham, Esq.   The Committee.

JUDGES.
Messrs. J. Page, W. G. Morse, R. O. Fordham.

STARTER (Blue and White).
W. A. Fordham, Esq.

COMMITTEE and CLERKS OF COURSE (Red).
Messrs. F. J. Bailey, V. Westrope, W. E. Bacon, A. H. Christy,
H. Bracey.

HON. SEC. (Light Blue).
Mr. Sam Parkhouse.

THE ASHWELL BRASS BAND
WILL PERFORM.

HARGEN, PRINTER, ROYSTON.

ASHWELL FLOWER SHOW
AND FETE

August Bank Holiday, August 7th
1939

PROGRAMME

P.M.
2. 0   Flower Show Tents open for inspection.
3. 0   Les Reartos (Sensational Acrobats and
       hand-to-hand balancers. Wonders in
       athletic ease).
3.30   Fancy Dress Parade and Judging.
4.20   Hitchin Junior Arts Club in Cabaret and
       Speciality Dances (under the direction of
       Miss Gladys Ingham).
5. 0   Fanshaw and Fern (Comedy Acrobatic
       knockabouts).
6. 0   Presentation of Flower Show Cups by
       C. H. Rigg, Esq.
6.15   Les Reartos (Second performance).
6.30   Hitchin Junior Arts Club (Second
       performance).
7. 0   Fanshaw and Fern (Second performance).
8. 0   Dancing on the Lawn.
9.45   Grand Display of Fireworks by H. Sullings,
       of Ipswich.

ASHWELL FOLK DANCERS will give displays of
Morris and Sword Dancing.

SEAGERS PUNCH & JUDY SHOW will entertain
during the afternoon and evening.

TENNIS TOURNAMENT on the Bury and
Elbrook House Courts.

By kind permission of Mrs. Wolverly Fordham, the
Bury Gardens will be open to visitors at a small
charge.

Music during the afternoon and evening by
ROYSTON TOWN BAND
The Band will play for Dancing on the Lawn at 8 p.m.
Public Address Equipment by Mr. W. E. Reeves, of Ashwell.

Teas and Buffet Refreshments under the
management of the Committee.
Licensed Refreshments by Mr. G. Knowles, of the
"Bushel and Strike," Ashwell.

KEEP THIS PROGRAMME—Prize given for lucky
number.
Price ONE PENNY.

ELPHICK, PRINTER, BIGGLESWADE.

Above: *A forerunner of the August Bank Holiday Show –
Thursday was early closing in 1890. The Sports Programme
included throwing the cricket ball; 100 yards handicap (1st prize:
a cruet stand). A married men's race 200 yards handicap (1st
prize: teapot); tug-of-war (prize: cask of Ale).* (Museum)

Right: *The 1939 Programme shows the number of attractions
brought in to entertain the crowd!* (Peter Howes)

Above: *Pony and Trap Parade 1949 Show.* (Albert Bush)

Above: *The large audience enjoying the Punch and Judy Show at what was probably the last show before the Second World War.* (Peter Howes)

Below: *The front and back cover of the first show after the Second World War.* (Nan Gerard)

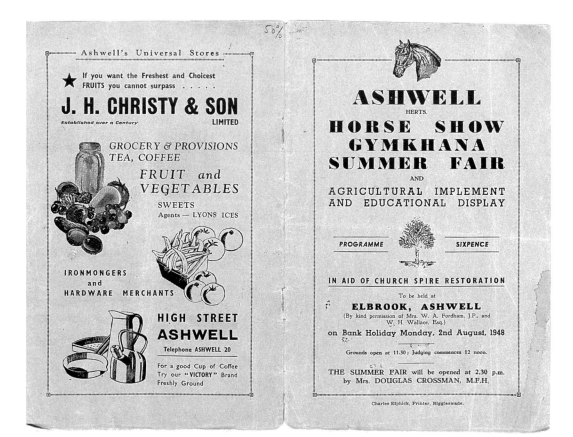

ASHWELL
HERTS.

HORSE SHOW
GYMKHANA
SUMMER FAIR
AND

AGRICULTURAL IMPLEMENT
AND EDUCATIONAL DISPLAY

PROGRAMME   SIXPENCE

IN AID OF CHURCH SPIRE RESTORATION

To be held at

ELBROOK, ASHWELL
(By kind permission of Mrs. W. A. Fordham, J.P., and
W. H. Wallace, Esq.)

on Bank Holiday Monday, 2nd August, 1948

Grounds open at 11.30 ; Judging commences 12 noon.

THE SUMMER FAIR will be opened at 2.30 p.m.
by Mrs. DOUGLAS CROSSMAN, M.F.H.

Charles Elphick, Printer, Biggleswade.

The Confutation of Wisdom by F. Sladen Smith and *The Dragon*, by Lady Gregory. Mrs. Raikes already owned a dragon costume and asked Mr. G. Whitby to furbish it up; he made new wings from the ribs of an old umbrella and feet from a pair of gardening gloves with wooden claws nailed to the figner-ends. Then whoever was due to play the dragon was taken ill and Mr. Whitby was coerced into wearing the costume himself. Later Mrs. Whitby became the WI's producer and one of their best actors.

The W.I. has continued to act plays, some of them specially written for it including one for the 50-year anniversary of the organisation in which Mrs. Williamson gave a wonderful performance as a slovenly housewife who was redeemed by the good offices of Mrs. Wallace as Fairy Denman (Denman College is W.I. Headquarters) and a large part of the membership played a dancing chorus in red-and-white gingham dresses and huge ,mob-caps. They have won several regional competitions. Other star commediennes included Mrs. Pitcher and the comedy team of Ruby Worboys and Ivy Capon.

The Merchant Taylors's School under Mr. Byles produced a musical play each year. A whole series of plays were performed there under Mr. and Mrs. Whitby, starting with a Christmas play in 1933, the year that they arrived. This was concocted by teachers and children together and concerned the goings-on of toys and ornaments brought to life on Christmas Eve by the Christmas-tree Fairy (Iris Street). There were also dolls and a teddy-bear and some tin soldiers. Mr. Whitby and the carpentry class made a giant clock, painted gold, ornamented with two ladies in white wigs and dressed with paniers, who danced a minuet with two gentlemen in knee-britches and lace-cuffed coats. Music was provided by the school orchestra.

Later an outdoor theatre was constructed in the garden. The stage was an artificial bank constructed over a rubbish-heap, with a background of elm trees, and the orchestra played in the summer-house. During the war, however, planes from the surrounding airfields flew over so frequently and noisily that the theatre was not usuable.

A Children's Theatre Club was started during the war by Mrs. Whitby, with the help of an evacuated teacher, Mrs. Crainford. They performed *Toad of Toad Hall*, and versions of *Rumpelstiltskin* and *Dick Whittington* specially written for them. At this time the comic stars of the group were Olive Andersen and Robert Sheldrick.

Twenty years later the Children's Theatre Club was revived by Kathy Hull and Marie Whitby. Plays for large groups of children being in short supply, those listed above were performed again; also a specially written version of *Alice Through the Looking Glass* and a review: *Professor Peanut's Round the World Show*. Later, Kathy Hull took over the group. Her productions included *The Sleeping Beauty*, *A Christmas Carol* and *The Wizard of Oz*.

Enthusiastic producers have several times started grown-up theatre groups. One of them was Peter Watt, from Odsey, who started a very successful group during the War. The stars of the group were Madge and Neville Howes, but there were a number of other excellent actors including Mr. Knowles (from the Bushell and Strike) who starred in Coward's *Fumed Oak*. Later they employed a professional producer, a refugee from Nazi persecution, named Katie Steinfeld.

She produced, among other plays, The *Winslow Boy*, *Blithe Spirits*, *The Chiltern Hundreds* and in 1948 what was possibly their best production, *Pygmalion*, with Dr. John Moynihan as Higgins and Dr. Sheila as his housekeeper.

The group eventually lapsed, but in 1976 Kathy Hull started the Ashwell Theatre Club. Their first production was a Victorian music-hall show which formed part of the celebrations of the centenary of the building of the big school-rrom at Merchant Taylors. Later they produced *Sailor Beware!* Other plays were *Bonaventure*, in which Sue Bain of Newnham both produced and played the lead, very successfully, *The Rivals* and a number of detective plays. The group also performed a number of pantomimes with notable success, and is still in existence, and going strong.

The Cast of "A Quiet Weekend", performed in the 1950's. L-R: Trevor Moore, Roger Howes, Margaret Bulley, Unknown, Dilys Hammond, Madge and Nevill Howes, Tom Pryor.

Some Ashwell People

Phyllis Fordham, John and Janet Beresford

Wolverley Fordham of Ashwell Bury married Phyllis Gribble of Henlow Grange in 1903. After a long honey moon, Phyllis Fordham settled into Ashwell village life, taking a keen interest in her gardens and the dilapidated farm houses and cottages, which she had restored during 1910 and 1911. In 1916, she and her husband moved into the Grange while the Bury became a Convalescent Home for wounded soldiers.

During this period John B Beresford, who was serving in the Forces, persuaded his wife, Janet, to leave London with their young children. Through an old school friend Janet came to see if Ashwell End house was suitable for the family. To her amazement she found that she was being interviewed by Phyllis, to see whether she was a suitable tenant for the house.

The test was passed and the two ladies became lifelong friends.

John Beresford was the author of several books and edited the Diary of a Country Parson. A tablet in Ashwell Church records his death. John Beresford was killed while on Civil Defence duties at the Treasury in 1940.

Janet settled at Ashwell End, joined many village bodies and like Phyllis Fordham was a keen supporter of the Liberal party. She died at Elmden, Essex in 1974, aged 83.

After Wolverley Fordham died in 1921 his widow employed Sir Edwyn Lutyens to remodel the Bury, then she became a churchwarden, Parish, Rural and County Councillor and supported every worthwhile cause in Ashwell, at the same time continuing the modernisation of her many properties. She died in 1958.

Albert contributes this reminiscence of Mrs Fordham, which illustrates the type of person she was:

> "It was round about 1950 when Brays modernised Butt Way cottages for her, bringing main drainage and electricity for the first time. We decided to work on the Oyston's house first because as it says in the Scriptures, Elsie was 'heavy with child'. In fact Arthur Baker, Eric Worboys and I worked until late one night to complete the bathroom and hot water system, and the baby girl was born a few hours later.
>
> Having fixed a sink in the kitchen, there was no room for a drainer because a huge brick copper filled the space. Elsie said Mrs Fordham wouldn't agree to take out the copper but I said I thought it could be arranged.
>
> So on the lady's next visit I guided her up the garden path, alongside three crude clothes posts. I said, "It's a great pity we can't give Elsie a drainer, because the copper is in the way". But she replied, "I have always wanted to get that copper out, the steam makes the kitchen unhealthy for all the children".
>
> Then while she summed up the situation her long tongue came out, and quite suddenly she said, "Each time I cycle past here I see these ugly clothes posts. Tell Elsie we will remove the copper on condition that she takes down the posts, which I will replace with some of those nice stone ones (concrete) in Bray's yard". Needless to say, we

removed the copper, a drainer was fixed, the concrete posts set up, for £5 Elsie bought a re-conditioned electric wash boiler and all was well again at Butt Way."

Albert's booklet, Fourpenny Phyllis, gives a much more comprehensive treatment of this village personality.

David Holbrook

David Holbrook grew up in Norwich, read English at Downing College, Cambridge, and at the age of 22 was wounded during the Normandy invasion. After the war, he worked on several journals before becoming involved in adult education and teaching. He has written more than 40 books, including 'Nothing Larger Than Life', which is a fictionalised account of his family's life at Ducklake, Ashwell.

In 1954, when he was appointed Tutor of the Bassingbourn Village College, with responsibility for evening classes and youth clubs in about a dozen Cambridgeshire villages, he and his wife, Margot, looked around for a house to rent. An upmarket estate agent told them of Ducklake at Ashwell to rent but only to a person with artistic leanings and one who would be useful in the village.

He qualified, of course, and the Holbrooks settled in with their two children, some geese, ducks and a swan on the river. They looked after the garden, which was checked frequently by the owner, Phyllis Fordham, who came round to hook out the odd nettle root with her walking stick spud.

David became a Parish Councillor. He obtained a grant for the Village Hall, started a Youth Club, wrote a number of books and poems and two more children were added to the family.

Three of the Holbrook children belonged to the Church Choir. David and the composer, Elizabeth Poston, were the authors of a cantata performed at the Ashwell Festival in 1968, the title of which was taken from the graffiti in Ashwell church - **m.ct.Xpenta.miseranda.ferox.violenta. m.cccl Superest plebs pessima testis infineque ventus Validus oc anno Maurus in orbe tonat m.ccclxi** - (Miserable, wild, distracted. 1350. A chastened people alone survives to witness: and in the end a tempest full mighty. This year, 1361, St Maur thunders in the world.)

The work, which was originally written and composed in 1961, was dedicated to the memory of Phyllis Fordham, 'without whose active interest much of Ashwell would have been spoiled long ago'.

In 1971, the Holbrooks moved to Devon, but the call of East Anglia was too strong and they moved to Cambridge in 1973, where they still live. David was Director of English Studies from 1981-88 at Downing College, where he is now Emeritus Fellow.

Sir William Gentle

The memorial service to the memory of Sir William Gentle, held at Norwich Cathedral in 1948, was attended by a large number of his friends and representatives of the many organisations to which he had belonged.

William Benjamin Gentle was born in 1864 at the Bushel & Strike in Mill Street, where his father, William Gentle, was the landlord.

Left: *Lord Walkden of Bookham, born in 1874 the son of Ashwell herbalist, Charles S. Walkden of philosophers gate fame, and Fordham brewery's Accountant. Lord Walkden became General Secretary of the Railway Clerks Association in 1907, Member of the T.U.C. Council 1921-36, M.P. for South Bristol 1921-31 and 1935-45. Elevated to the peerage in 1945. (John M. Pollock)*

William Reeves, one of Ashwell's interesting personalities. Married Nora Thorne in 1929 and came to live in Pleasant Place, Ashwell. A successful businessman, he installed the first T.V. set in Ashwell in 1938 and developed a firm with a high reputation as electrical contractors. Parish and Rural District Councillor, Museum helper and involved in many worthy village causes. Died 1976. (Nora Reeves)

Edric Cundell, well known as a composer and conductor, was Principal of the Guildhall School of Music from 1938. In 1958, soon after his retirement he came to live at Bear House, and was a great a supporter of the Ashwell Festival. He died in 1961. (Anthony Catterick)

Ethel Dilley, another great Ashwell personality, who now lives in Wolverley House. Widowed, with six children, you can read about her exploits elsewhere in this book. (Ethel Dilley)

Below:*A photograph of an 'open' plane in which she is pictured with Charles Haylock and which she flew as a 'pleasure flight' on a seaside trip in the early 1920's. (Ethel Dilley)*

Above Right: *John Morris was born in 1913. He was educated at Rossall School and Jesus College, Oxford. After six years in the army he made a career as an historian, becoming Leon Fellow of London University and later took his Ph.D. John Morris came to live at Little Garth , Mill Street with his wife Susan and their four children in 1966. It was while he was working on the text and translation of the Domesday Book that the B.B.C. came to interview him. Finding that Ashwell was a Domesday Borough, they decided to film not only John at work, but the village as well. John Morris died in 1977 with only part of his work completed. Susan Morris well known for her pottery and now lives in High Street, told me that John loved the space and peace that he found at Little Garth, while from 1966 to 1973 he was working on, what he considered his special contribution, as an historian. The work he cared most about was "The Age of Arthur"'. (Susan Morris)*

Edward "Bill" Gray, Phyllis Fordham's chauffeur and right hand man for 56 years to 1958. In her will she left him £250. (Mrs. D Berry)

Peter Moynihan was born in Ashwell in 1933, the eldest son of Drs John and Sheila Moynihan. Following University at Oxford he moved to London. Although most of his work was in or connected with the theatre he became a household name when he landed the role of "Philip" in the long-running "Life with Katie" OXO advertisement scenes, playing alongside Mary Holland as "Katie" his screen wife, with whom he is shown here. (Ross Moynihan)

Below: With her brother Sid Waldock Mrs. Bullard at 96 one of Ashwell's oldest inhabitants, awarded a silver watch for 5 years perfect attendance at Ashwell School. Never had an illness or went into hospital until 1992 with a broken wrist. Bill Hardyman, the chap in the centre is Ashwell's oldest man at 98.

Right: Robert Skerman, well-known in Ashwell as the "bouncer" Robert loves to bounce a ball as he walks through the village. Also known for his habit of shutting garden gates and being generally helpful. (Museum)

After serving in South Africa with the Cape Mounted Rifles, the Metropolitan and Reading police, he was Chief Constable of Brighton from 1901-1920, during which time he was created a Knight of Grace of the Order of St John of Jerusalem in England, in 1916.

Both King Edward VII and Winston Churchill were interested in his Police Instruction book, his guide to the Children's Act and the scheme for helping the poor children of Brighton. Ending his police career in 1920, Sir William acquired an amusement park at Manchester, was a pioneer of greyhound racing, Managing Director of Brighton Palace Pier and a director of the London General Omnibus Company. He was High Sheriff of Norfolk in 1938, Mayor of Thetford for many years, Hon Freeman of the Borough of Thetford, had Queen Victoria, King George V and King George VI medals, was a JP, a Norfolk County Councillor, Commissioner for Income Tax and High Steward of Norwich Cathedral. Sir William was also a frequent visitor to Ashwell, where one of his Rolls Royce cars was often seen at the Ashwell Show or the Merchant Taylors' School where, in the early 1900s, he presented a silver challenge cup and of course he had electric light installed in the church and in 1930 paid for the restoration of the museum.

Percy Sheldrick

The Sheldrick Family, and indeed many other people, always regarded Uncle Percy as a bit of an eccentric, as of course he was. From an early age he became an expert needleman, which in the early part of the century was regarded as woman's work. However, Ashwell men, who during World War I were in the trenches with Percy, have told how, when volunteers were needed to fetch in badly wounded men from beyond the barbed wire, Percy was the first to volunteer, until he too was severely wounded and sent home, never able to do normal work again.

So with his knowledge of needlework he was soon accepted into a tapestry school for disabled servicemen and went on from there to become a master weaver at the William Morris Tapestry Works at Merton Abbey until he left in 1939. During the Second World War, Percy did clerical work in Letchworth. After the war, he not only worked at home embroidering samplers, banners and other pieces, using embroidery wools, Bruges silks and gold thread, but took classes in embroidery at Ashwell Further Education Centre and at Hitchin and was invited to speak on the subject to pupils in five counties.

An exhibition of Percy's work was opened by Lady Bowes Lyon at the Further Education Centre in the early seventies, followed by another exhibition at Hitchin Library, and an exhibition of his work was on tour in the United States for some time. Many of the banners and other needlework in Ashwell church were made by Percy. Apart from his work, Uncle Percy was a devout churchman and verger for a number of years. He died in 1978.

In 1976, at the age of 85 and in failing health, Percy was taken in a wheelchair to meet the Merchant Taylors, on their visit to mark the Centenary of the Re-opening of the Merchant Taylors' School. He said, "Time seems so unimportant, the past is gone, today is here and we have no idea what tomorrow will bring".

Ashwell Allsorts

The ownership of Ashwell Springs

For years the ownership of the Springs had been of great concern to many people. At the 1949 Parish meeting the Council admitted that although they had maintained the Springs for many years, they did not know who the owners were.

It was known that many years ago Fordhams had taken possession of one spring by piping it from the point where it left the chalk by an iron pipe below the bed of the river and into the brewery to make their well-known beers. There was also the question of the mill rights. The brewers owned the mill and it is said that by ancient law the owner of a mill had the water rights back, in this case to the springs.

In September 1951 the Council decided to leave the matter in the hands of Mr W H Fordham. One local argument seems to have been that whereas the Springs had been in that hollow since time immemorial, the Fordham family had only come to Ashwell in the last century.

In 1952 it was said, 'discussions are taking place re the ownership of the Springs, and it is hoped there will be a successful outcome'.

In 1965, while it was decided to improve the steps down to the Springs, there was still great concern as it was rumoured that Whitbreads might put the Springs up for sale, although the Parish Council still thought they belonged to the parish. Someone suggested that a seat was needed at the Springs. In 1966 Lee Valley Water Company asked for a licence to abstract 1,750 gallons of water daily from a borehole at Slip End. Would it dry up the Springs? Still in 1966 legal beagle, Geoffrey Coad, said, "I hope the matter of ownership of the springs will be finalised by March 1967." Whitbreads offered some land in addition to the Springs basin in 1968. The Parish Council accepted. In 1970, a set of ten rules for the management of Ashwell Springs was drawn up (getting nearer!), followed by a number of concrete stepping stones, made by Geoffrey Coad and friends, and lowered into the Springs basin, so that old and young could cross over with dry feet. In 1972, the wooden seat, suggested in 1965, arrived, the gift of the Ashwell Show Committee.

After many difficulties, the issue of the Springs' ownership was resolved. At a special ceremony on 9 May 1973, attended by Councillors P Milton, Eric Gurney, Howard Day, Jeremy Fordham, Sam Wallace, Dr Fergus Moynihan, Gurney Sheppard, Philip Crump, John Bray and Whitbread Director, William H Fordham, Solicitor, Geoffrey Coad and representatives of Whitbreads Brewery, the deed was handed over and Ashwell Springs returned to Ashwell.

The Cottage Garden

Ashwell's post lady for over 60 years, Flo Worboys will long be remembered in the village; no matter whether the weather was wet or fine, she went cheerfully on her way, pushing or riding her bicycle.

On her retirement in 1987, the postmaster said that Flo had cycled 200,000 miles, the equivalent of six times round the world, delivering the mail. Now her family have given a seat to the cottage garden in her memory, just a few yards from the cottage where she had spent most of her life and raised that family.

Flo, who was honoured by Queen Elizabeth in 1989 with the BEM and later met Her Majesty at the opening of the Letchworth Leisure Centre, would have remembered the row of dingy cottages which stood on this spot until about 1924, built right against the street with a narrow back yard containing three privies.

Flo would also have remembered one of the families who lived there: Alf and Hannah Seaby, with their four sons and one daughter. Alf, who worked at Westbury Farm, was quite a character. In those days, farmworkers stopped at 10.00 am to have their 'beaver'. Alf always had a quarter loaf of bread and a hunk of red cheese. Before 1939, when we were proud to be British, we enjoyed our red or off-white cheese, and the upper crust their Stilton, Gorgonzola, etc, which are still made. There are now 125 different kinds of British cheese.

Out in the fields, Alf's midday meal, every other day, consisted of a pork and onion dumpling tied up in the cloth in which it had been boiled (not to be confused with a 'Bedfordshire Clanger', which had meat at one end and jam at the other). The pieces of pork Alf tied up in the cloth to be re-used in the next dumpling - presumably to give it a bit of flavour! Hannah found it very hard to get up on cold, frosty mornings. One such morning, Alf took one of the Westbury horses to Bean's the Blacksmiths to be shod, and seeing all the chimneys in Swan Street smoking except his, he slipped in and shouted up the stairs, "Fire! Fire!". "Where, Alf?" cried Hannah, as she hurried down the stairs in her flannelette nightie. "In everybody's bloody house except ours!", replied Alf, as he hurried away to collect his horse.

After the cottages were demolished and the site cleared, Albert Skerman, who lived in the cottage next to Flo, took it over, growing all kinds of plants and cuttings which, over the years, grew into a fine old English cottage garden until 1968, when the owner of the land had plans prepared for a rather unsuitable house to be built on the site. After several emergency meetings, £2,000 was raised by a group of interested people and the garden was saved; at first it was suggested that it be included in the Museum Trust, but eventually it was vested in the Hertfordshire Buildings Preservation Trust. In 1983, the Trust sold the nearby cottage. Then, after some persuasion, a share of the proceeds of the sale was given to the Ashwell Village Trust. The layout of the garden was changed to make it easier for Albert Chandler, Philip Crump, Liz Moynihan and other helpers to keep it tidy, but at the same time attractive to both visitors and Ashwellians. The aims of the trust are to preserve the character of Ashwell for the people of the village and the general public.

Ashwell Quarries Nature Reserve

Is administered by the Hertfordshire and Middlesex Trust for Nature Conservation under the terms of a management agreement signed in 1972. It is a closed reserve but access is by permit on application to the Trust or the wardens Christine and Trevor James, 56 Brook Street, Ashwell. Volunteers meet on certain

BACK

Above: *Marie Whitby's valiant efforts to keep Ashwell's streets clean are told elsewhere in this book.* (Evening Post, January 20, 1973)

Goosey Lucy. During the 1940's whilst stationed at the Maltings, Jock McBeale met and married milk girl May Bryant; they raised a family of four and after the war Jock found work nearby. One day he brought home a gosling hoping to fatten it up for Christmas. The goose named Goosey Lucy was partial to a drop of Jock's beer and after being taken for a walk round the lanes, would often wander off by herself. The children saved Lucy from the oven and she lived to a good age. Goosey Lucy is shown here with Jock and the youngest daughter Kate. (Mavis Fox, nee McBeale)

The Women's Institute, in 1969 were so annoyed at the filthy state of the streets, weighed in with their efforts. (W.I. Photograph Album)

The above are a group people who over the years have been involved with the Thrift Shop, celebrating its 21st Anniversary. It started in November 1969, opened in an old poultry shed in Peter Sheldrick's premises on Station road. At first only good quality worn clothing was accepted for sale. Later the Thrift Shop moved into the Village Hall kitchen and the goods on display apart from clothing, included household goods and toys. The owner of the goods when sold, received 80% of the selling price, the remainder was retained to be given to the various charities which the committee had approved. Over the years many well known Ashwell people have worked at the Thrift Shop keeping it open on Monday afternoons, and thousands of pounds have been donated to a number of good causes since 1969. (Royston Crow)

Above: *Mrs. Evelyn Brown delivers the first "Meals on Wheels" in 1967, accompanied by the Organiser.* (Mrs. E. Brown)

Left: *Pat Coad and Liz Moynihan in the Cottage Garden.* (Royston Crow)

Sundays clearing scrub, mowing and haymaking. Many rare flowers have reappeared.

There was a lime kiln here until about 1930, Nathaniel Salmon, in 1728 wrote of two small edifices 'They are built of stone, of which a quarry affords in Ashwell field just by'. Ashwell Field is part of the Westbury farm lands, which were farmed by the Christy family for several centuries. The farm is now part of the estate of Jeremy Fordham, whose family have been landowners in Hertfordshire for 400 years.

Memories of Ashwell

Among the letters we received after the publication of "A different world" was a very interesting one from Margaret Bulley which almost fully takes in the period this book covers.

Margaret came to Ashwell when she was six in 1939 and stayed until 1972. Her father was blind.

Her narrative proceeds:

"My father and mother were placed in Pembroke Farm by the Herts Society for the Blind, who rented it for six years before buying it from a Miss Taylor. She had bought the farm as a weekend retreat and the loft above the stables was completely fitted out with a dance floor, electric heaters and lights with Christmas decorations still up when we arrived. Everywhere was derelict and Mr George Bean at the Slip End cottages helped my parents get it straight. We were there from 1939 to 1972. Miss Taylor used to race cars at Brooklands and I used to play on a burnt out one which she had left behind the buildings.

"Mrs Wolverley Fordham was connected with the Herts Society for the Blind and used to come on her 'sit-up-and-beg bicycle' to see them. One day my mother was in the village shopping and Mrs Fordham asked her if she had seen her bicycle, as she couldn't remember where she had left it. When it was election time, she would send her big black car with her chauffeur, Mr Gray, to take them to vote. She also sent her farm manager, Mr Wallace, to give them any advice he could.

"Fred Pettingell, who used to be the road foreman, worked for my father part-time until he died. He biked up to the farm one day a week and he used to whistle all the time he was working. My mother fetched him up in the car in later years and, just before he died, he was found in the village in the early hours of the morning expecting my mother to pick him up, having no idea of the time. I remember, as a little girl, when he was working down the lane with his gang, my dog wet up one of the men's legs. I was very embarrassed.

"Lottie and Charlie Bird: Lottie was my mother's helper for over twenty years. She would cycle up to the farm one day a week to help mother. We kept lodgers, first, from the Wallington Radio Station, then people who came from London to get away from the bombing. Mrs Bird always had her dinner with us and, one day, she got her false teeth mixed up in the treacle pudding. We did laugh. Sometimes I'd cycle to Baldock cinema with her.

"Westrope's man used to come to collect our grocery order and later they were delivered. Day's the bakers would deliver the bread, Crump's the fish and Dennis the meat. Mr Taylor from Baldock would bring ice cream made at Letchworth Bacon Factory and, later fish and chips. My parents only had a pony and trap in those days. Flo Worboys used to deliver the mail with her bicycle and did a sterling job as her round was Odsey, Baldock road, Slip End and our farm. Clive Whitby used to come and help with the hoeing.

"Miss Lilian Bryant was Head teacher at Odsey School where I used to go, and cycled in all weathers, hardly missing a day. Miss Brooks was the infant teacher and came on the train from Cambridge every day. They let us sit round the open fire on cold winter days with our 1/3 pint of free milk warming in the hearth. We were allowed to bring our coats in to warm before the fire before we went home. In the summer, we used to carry our desks out into the playground. I can remember Miss Bryan asking who had a three-speed bicycle. I said I had. She took the whole class round to the bike shed to see it and I hadn't got one. I thought she said 'free speed', and I could go any speed I liked. I hasten to add I was only eight at the time.

"Miss Spencer lived at Odsey Grange, Mrs K Watts next door and Mrs Spencer at Odsey Corner. Willie Fordham lived in the big house in the fields and I and others were caught stealing walnuts there. He came to the school and we all had stained fingers.

"I can remember the rubber dump at Ashwell Station, and the Italian prisoners of war were very good to us children. My parents were very good friends of Rolly and Alice Worboys and we would go in the pony and trap to play cards and have supper with them. They were also friends with Mr and Mrs Bert King, who would walk up from the village on a Saturday afternoon to have tea, then my mother would take them back in the car. One day we were having tea and there was a terrible gale. A slate blew off their roof and went right through the roof of the car. When we got to the top of the hill near the old farm buildings we had to stop and remove bales of straw from the road, and the drive into the farm was cut off by broken telephone wires.

"I remember 'Shaver' very well. He was the brother of Mrs Bean at Pembroke cottages. He would visit her every Christmas and we would borrow his pram to play 'Mothers and Fathers'. He drank meths and would swap bread with the old Cat Lady, who would stay in my father's straw shed for a few days. She had lots of cats and kittens under chicken wire in her pram and wore broken plimsolls in all weathers. It was said that she owned three big properties in Cambridge.

"I knew Mr and Mrs Neville Howes, as I was a member of the Ashwell Players. "We also used to buy apples at the barn in the village at one penny a pound. My father would take me to Morley's, the bakers, for a cream bun and have a haircut opposite. "I hope this is of interest to you. My father is now 85 and, although he can't walk very well and of course is blind, his memory is still good.

Many thanks once again for your delightful book.

Yours sincerely

Margaret Langley (nee Bulley)"

The Dixies Stone

Partly buried in the grass verge near Dixies Farmhouse in High Street, is the Dixies Stone. Archaeologists in the past decided that the stone is either a boulder from the clay or it is of millstone grit. There have been several theories as to its purpose. Henry Bowman suggested that a few mysterious marks on it were runes, the language of some ancient folk, others thought that the earliest inhabitants of Ashwell brought it here as some sort of religious symbol and built their village round it.

From his relatives, Henry had been told that in 1840, after complaints had been made about the stone being a nuisance, (at that time it was actually in the street) farmer, Tommy Chapman, with horses and chains pulled the Dixies stone into Dixies farmyard. Whereupon the vicar, being somewhat of an antiquarian, had a fence erected around the spot where the stone had stood. The fence only made matters worse.

Then followed a war of words between farmer, parson and squire, Edward King Fordham. The squire won and had the stone removed from the farmyard and taken to protect the corner of an old cottage just outside the brewery entrance. So it became the Mill Street stone until the cottage was demolished and a new one erected on the spot adjoining the also newly built brewery offices. Once more the stone was moved, this time into Ashwell Bury stable yard where it was used by the Fordhams to mount their horses, and there it rested, almost forgotten, until the Second World War. Ashwell, like most towns and villages in the United Kingdom, had formed its own little army, known at first as Local Defence Volunteers and later as The Home Guard. Mr William Herbert Fordham, a director of the family brewery, who had served as an office in the 1914-18 war, was enrolled as one of the officers in charge. Later, at a time when the war was going badly for the Allies and there was fear of invasion, Captain Fordham got his troop together to roll the Dixies stone down to the mill bridge from where it could be rolled into the road to hinder the Nazi tanks as they rumbled round Cow Lane in a bid to invade Ashwell. Fortunately for all of us, this did not come to pass.

So the stone rested against a fence until Saturday, 13 November, 1948 when, after correspondence with the Parish and County Councils, permission was given for the seven hundredweight stone to be brought back to its present and we hope permanent resting place. With his Dixies Farm tractor and trailer, Maurice Brown, Fred Bray and several strong helpers, we brought it back, dug a hole and according to instructions from County buried one third of the stone in the roadside and surrounded it with concrete.

Ashwell's fire brigade (AS)

Ashwell has had more than its fair share of fires. One of the first recorded in the churchwardens' records was in 1622, then in 1632 the clerk recorded, "Given to divers labourers whiche did work all night at the fire. XXVId.". Then in 1660 the parish bought a fire engine. 'To a hand engeon to throw water. 8s"2d. Paid carriage of it from London. 1s"4d.' Ashwell always had a fire brigade of sorts. I remember in the 1920s it consisted of ten or a dozen volunteers who were always on call for any fire which might occur in the village. Their names were printed on cards which were on display at various points in the village. Their equipment consisted of a long length of canvas hose and a brass tube which could be connected to any of the hydrant points in the water main. The hose and tube were stacked on a red painted two-wheeled cart which was kept on the premises of George Strickland in Silver Street.

I remember seeing the brigade in action late one Sunday morning in either 1931 or 1932, having been called to a chimney fire at a cottage in Gardiners Lane, which was occupied by a young RAF man from Henlow who was married to an Ashwell girl.

Fortunately, several of the firemen were supping Simpson's beer in The Rose and Crown, so were more or less on the spot; while two of the men dashed off to fetch the handcart, the others found ladders. The hydrant and hose were quickly fixed while one of the firemen rushed up the ladders and thrust the hose through the black smoke well down the chimney, the hydrant was turned on full blast, so full in fact that it not only washed out the flames but washed the soot and some of the family's bits and pieces through the front door into the street. The family had to find other accommodation for a few days until the cottage dried out.

After George Strickland died, the fire handcart and hose was housed at the cage, the Parish lock-up in Hodwell. At that time no one knew of the trouble that fire equipment was going to cause between Ashwell and the Hitchin Rural District Council.

Soon after war was declared in 1939, the Ashwell Auxiliary Fire Service was set up and supplied with a fire trailer pump; at the same time the old Parish handcart and hose were taken away.

In 1941, the trailer pump disappeared and the Clerk to the Parish Council wrote a letter to the Hitchin RDC, demanding its return, especially as the Council considered the pump more essential than ever, in view of the large quantities of lard now stored in the centre of the village. The trailer pump was returned.

At the Council meeting of 1 July, 1942, the Ashwell Auxiliary Fire Service requested a site for a Nissen hut and a gateway with a runway down to the Springs. The Council approved the access to the Springs, but thought the Nissen hut and its site were the responsibility of the National Fire Service. In October, however, the Council agreed to spend £14 1s. 5d. on ballast, cement and railway sleepers, including labour (16 men) to prepare the runway. In October, 1943, the District Council refused to reimburse the money and the fire trailer pump had once more disappeared. The Fire Service Chief said that as Ashwell's fire equipment (the handcart and hose) was handed over to the Rural District Council, it was not in his power to return it. A very strong letter was sent to the RDC with a demand for the return of at least some of the fire fighting equipment, but with little effect.

The Annual Parish Meeting was well attended in 1957 when two officers of the Fire Service gave a lecture on fire fighting, probably due to the fact that a mother and child had been burned to death in the cottage nearest the Church in Church Path. On this tragic occasion, the husband tripped over a paraffin heater on the ground floor, its flames shooting up the stairs, making rescue impossible from inside. Byron Searle, then living in Church Lane, and Charlie Meckin rushed down to the scene and tried to rescue the victims by ladder but the heat was too fierce. The gravestone reads, 'Violet Harvey aged 34 and Rita Joy aged 5 died together Jan 10 1957'.

The only suggestions made were that every householder should have some fire fighting equipment.

Another fire caused by paraffin resulted in another tragedy in 1959. Mrs Toombs, a part-time postlady, died in a cottage in Gardiners Lane when her husband was away. Philip Crump's efforts to get in to rescue her were thwarted as the door was jammed.

The nearest fire stations then were at Baldock, Letchworth and Royston. Ashwell never got its hose and handcart back.

During the Firemen's strike in 1977, Ashwell organised a team of volunteer firemen, rather like the pre-war fire brigade. At the first news of a fire, Phil Crump would dash over to the Church and ring the fire bell to warn the fire fighters to hurry to the spot where their equipment was housed. This consisted of a red lorry loaned by Gurney Sheppard which was loaded with hosepipes, shovels, ladders and all the necessary gear to fight a fire. The Rector, the Rev John Mullett, was particularly concerned about the old folk in the village, following the death of Mrs Phyllis Dellar, who had been found dead in her smoke-filled cottage opposite the Recreation Ground in 1977.

Two years earlier, there had been a serious fire at Redbourn Plastics' Factory in Ashwell Street. Fortunately, this had not involved any loss of life but, as in a later fire in the Wiles' home in West End, the damage was extensive.

Ashwell's blizzards

Being on the western edge of the Anglian region and only just about in the South East, Ashwell basically enjoys a fairly equable climate, a reasonable ration of sunshine and a rainfall averaging 24 inches a year.

Since 1976, Peter Bryant has kept meticulous records of rainfall and temperature, taking over from Bill Wallace, thus continuing a very valuable service.

Snow has always been Ashwell's biggest hazard and, when whipped up by strong winds, it does not need a heavy fall of the white stuff to block every entrance to the village.

Albert remembers the blizzard of March 1916. Although Ashwell lies more or less in a valley, it did not escape the fierce winds which sent snow swirling through the village, blocking all roads and uprooting between 300 and 400 trees. One of Fordham's brewery wagons, on the journey home was stopped by fallen trees on the road from the A1 to Newnham. The drayman had to decide whether to stay with the horses and probably freeze to death, or unharness the horses and attempt to get them over the fields to Ashwell, which of course he did.

The next day, the folks turned out to inspect the damage. Albert went to see his grandfather and Peter Skerman cutting up trees in Cow Lane with a cross-cut saw. Along the North Field road, where the farm buildings known as 'The Pump' used to be, trees torn up by the roots lay across the road like ninepins. They were later sawn up and moved by German prisoners but the tree roots, still encrusted with soil, lay like giant mushrooms tipped on edge for at least 30 or 40 years.

In January 1940, Norman Gurney and his school friends waited outside Christy's in falling snow for the 8.15 am Eastern National double decker bus to take them to school. By the time the bus arrived - late due to the weather - the snowstorm had increased in intensity and at the foot of Newnham Way the bus stopped, stuck in a deep snowdrift. For another week it was impossible to get out of Ashwell and then only by a single track cutting through 15 feet drifts.

The winter of 1947 was another severe one, with the blizzard of 5 March blocking every road out of the village. But ready for an emergency of this kind, Herts County Council's roads department had about 20 shovels stored at Dixies Farm. They were loaned out to a gang of men supervised by Road Foreman, Fred Pettingell. The gang concentrated mainly on Newnham road, the road used by bus loads of workers on their way to Letchworth and other towns, and Station road, for those people going to the station or on to Royston.

On 16 March there was a tremendous gale. The high winds whipped the snow off the fields and onto the roads; the area was deep in snow for weeks on end. Dr John Moynihan borrowed a Landrover to visit outlying districts.

All building work was stopped by the constant freezing. Bray's were luckier than most builders. Practically all stocks of building materials had been used up during the war, especially timber and now, like some foodstuffs, it was rationed just at a time when a quantity of timber was needed for concrete shuttering at Bluegates Farm.

However, Mrs Fordham was persuaded to allow Bray's to take sufficient floorboards and other timbers for shuttering from the derelict Page's brewery at West End. Then, seeing the sorry skeleton of the buildings, she decided to demolish the lot, after salvaging any useful materials. Geoffrey Whitby, the headmaster of the Merchant Taylors' school, had earlier suggested that the cellars, some ten feet deep, might be converted into a swimming pool for the village but due to lack of funds that never happened. So 107 years after Sale and Christy had built their brewery, apart from the Maltings which became the Village Hall and the Stable Block, the Scout Hut, it was wiped off the face of Ashwell.

In order to preserve that section of extensive cellars, which extend under the grounds of Westbury House, the builders bricked up the arches, below the boundary wall, then dropped the claybat walls of the buildings directly into the cellars, over which soil was laid, thus forming the garden of Westbury cottage.

During that long winter, there was an acute shortage of coal, causing many factories to shut down. Food rationing at wartime levels was re-imposed and the meat ration reduced to 1/- a week.

But the freezing conditions of the winter were followed by a glorious summer.

The sixties stopped swinging for a time in 1962 when, on Boxing Day, once again high winds and snow isolated Ashwell from the civilised world and severe frost caught many people out. Norman Gurney crashed his Dormobile on a hill in Luton, injuring his wife, Ruby. All roads were blocked, but this time the County Council had arranged with the farmers to keep the roads clear by using their tractors with snow ploughs attached. Even so, a double decker bus was stranded along the Newnham road and the load of school children and work people were left to battle their way home through the snow drifts and it was still necessary for the shovel gang to turn out.

Elbrook House flats were frozen solid and the tenants were kept busy cooking their sausages and bacon over a bonfire in the yard until the flats were thawed out. Dozens of Ashwell's outside toilets were frozen up and when eventually the thaw came, the local builders' merchants soon sold out of cisterns and lavatory pans.

Since 1975 and 1976, when we had quite severe winters with a lot of snow, we have had no repetition of the great freeze ups of the forties and sixties.

Ashwell Women's Institute

The Women's Institute has played a very important part in the life of the village since it started in 1918.

We have been fortunate to be able to examine their scrap book compiled in 1953 and 1954, and it contains a typically painstaking treasury of information on Ashwell, winning third prize in the 1954 Women's Institute competition, being commended on 'the scholarly research that had been put into it'. Mrs Edith Camp and Mrs Evelyn Brown were the main compilers, with the help of other members.

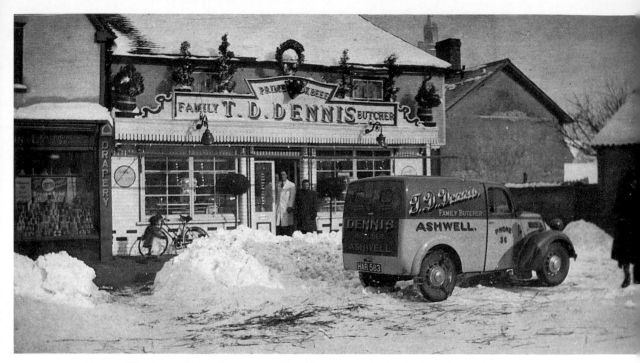

The terrible winter of 1947 demonstrated by this photograph of T. D. Dennis Butchers. Tommy can be seen in the doorway (Pearl Williams nee Glasscock)

Snowballs on Newnham Hill 1947, Betty Gentle, Queenie Eversden, Mollie Bryant. (Mollie Bryant)

Right: Winter in 1962. (Nancy Eversden)

Left: Albert Sheldrick clearing the snow at 90 High St, after the 1962 blizzard. (Ann Nally)

The Nally family lived at Ringstead while the late Jim Nally was here in the U.S. Forces.

The wide range of the activities is demonstrated by some extracts from the Minute books. The first extracts show how much the WI contributed to the war effort, especially in a welfare sense.

In 1939, Mrs Walter Bray suggested that a sewing class be formed among school children to do sewing and mending for the evacuees in the village. The WI held a whist drive for the fund for blinded soldiers. Mark Crump explained the way to cook cheap cuts of meat while Mrs Revels won the prize for the best meat dish to cost not more than ninepence.

In the same year, five hundredweight of sugar was ordered (for preserving fruit and making jam) from the National Federation of WIs.

In 1940, 167 surgical coats were made in 10 days for the Red Cross, and Dr Sheila Moynihan spoke very emphatically on the menace to the morals of our girls, and the young soldiers in our midst at the present time, and implored members to do all that lay in their power to enable them to preserve the sanctity of courtship and marriage. In October the Agricultural secretary announced that 3,179 lbs of preserves were made at the local preserving centre, and 16 hundredweight of sugar had been used. Mrs Seymour had kindly stored the sugar at Little Garth.

At the January 1941 meeting, members were urged to join the War Savings movement and were told that Oaklands would send an expert to cull their chickens so that no poultry food would be wasted on unprofitable hens. At the October meeting, members had invited a few soldiers who were at the Army School in the Maltings for a programme of games and "turns" but on the night nearly 100 turned up. In some miraculous way large quantities of food were found. The soldier guests asked if they might join the WI! During War Weapons Week the WI were responsible for a 'Messerschmitt', which was on view? At the 1941 Christmas party, members were asked to take an active part in Warship Week and a talk was given on Civil Defence by Dr Sheila and members gave in their names, offering to do useful work in case of invasion.

In July 1942 members were asked to collect herbs for medicinal and culinary use. At the September meeting it was decided to make toys in aid of the Red Cross Prisoner of War Fund. £9,000 was raised by the Herts WI.

At the June 1943 meeting, Mrs Beresford said she had some pamphlets on Venereal Disease which she would be happy to lend. A talk was given on the USA and members were asked to offer hospitality to American soldiers. At the August meeting members were asked to bring an onion to the next meeting; these would be sent to the Red Cross who would sell them to the Government, who would then send them to the Royal Navy and Merchant Navy.

Members collected half a hundredweight of onions for the Navy, but the powers-that-be decided that it was not sufficient to bother with. Ashwell & Hinxworth Women's Institutes in 1943 raised £123 0s 7d from the sale of toys for the Red Cross Prisoner of War Fund.

In April 1944 arrangements were made for a social to be held during 'Salute the Soldier Week', and there was a demonstration on meatless meals, Bean Roll, Vegetable Charlotte and Savoury Omelette.

During this year the members held a "Pageant of the Shawls" which was a great success. Miss Anne Hyslop, in her little book about Ashwell, wrote an account of this event, and we quote extracts:

The pageant of shawls

"There are in many of our homes old shawls, lovingly preserved, which seldom see the light of day and I am sure their owners often say, 'What a pity we do not use these shawls today'. But during the war years on one occasion, these old shawls had one more hour of glorious life, when they were brought out of their hiding places and were seen in a 'Pageant of Shawls', held in the Bury Garden on August Bank Holiday in 1944. Amongst the most beautiful of old shawls are the soft woollen shawls of Kashmir. The introduction of such shawls into this country was greatly encouraged by young soldiers and builders of empire, who sent lovely Indian shawls home as presents. It was the Kashmir shawl, embroidered in pine designs, which the Scottish weavers of Paisley imitated so successfully on their looms and which lead to the popularity of the Paisley shawls.

Many of these beautiful shawls were on show, worn by their proud owners. A tableau was shown of a company of Ashwell ladies in Victorian dress. Mrs Wallace wore the purple silk dress and black lace shawl of her great-grandmother. By her side was a girl wearing the Victorian dress of a young girl of the period with a lovely scarf shawl of white silk embroidered with flowers, and more than a hundred years old. Mrs Wallace was seated on a chair, made, worked and presented to the original wearer of the purple dress as a wedding present. The Beresford Bearing robe was on show, made of bright red satin edged with gold lace and worn by all the Beresford babies since the middle of the 17th century. Miss Wylie showed a variety of Scottish shawls. Miss Christine Angell in Welsh national dress, showed a long grey shawl and tall black hat. There was an Irish colleen in her green shawl and a lassie from Lancashire in shawl and clogs. There were country shawls, soft and warm, worn at weddings, christenings and funerals a hundred years ago, silk embroidered Indian shawls, which had belonged to the late Mrs Critchley and sent to her by her uncle, General Snow, from India. The wearers of the shawls were seen on the flat roof of the Bury. One girl wore a Quaker dress and bonnet and long grey shawl. She slipped through the door of the drawing room and took the hand of a young American soldier from Bassingbourn, in token of the friendship between our country and the USA."

In January 1945 the meeting voted to carry on jam making during the war, but not after (they had had enough), and in February the winner of the most darned garment was Mrs Jack Ashby. In August there was a Help For Holland scheme. It was announced that there were large bales of useful articles ready for collection. Miss Hyslop read a letter from Queen Wilhelmina of the Netherlands conveying her thanks and appreciation.

At the January 1946 meeting it was decided to start a clothing stall to help liberated countries, and a talk entitled 'Germany in the last days of the war' was given by Albert Sheldrick.

Due to rationing, no food was served at the July 1946 meeting. The members voted against the extension of Summertime throughout the year. It was announced that the jam which had been received from the Queensland Women's Federation would be raffled. A talk was then given by Mr Bosworth Monk on 'The Atomic Age', explaining how years of research had resulted in the atom bomb which was dropped on Japan, the ability to use it for peaceful purposes and the awful prospect of another war. Draw tickets for the jam received from Australia were distributed by means of lucky numbers as were the contents of a further parcel received from Australia. London Garden Scheme: it was agreed to join in with the rest of Hertfordshire and adopt the Borough of Tottenham. Plants would be collected in October for dispatch. Mrs Fordham kindly placed the stables at the disposal of the packers, supervised by Mrs A Sheldrick. At the November meeting a scheme for Sitters In was agreed and several members gave in their names as willing sitters in. Mrs Webb, the National Savings Organiser,

Above and Right:
*Members of the Ashwell
Women's Institute
celebrate their Golden
Jubilee at a special dinner
in 1968.*

Below: *Members of the
W.I. Choir (1969) which
performed so successfully.*
(These three
photographs come from
the W.I. collection)

CUP FOR ¹⁹⁶⁹
ASHWELL

This is Ashwell WI Choir
which won a cup for the
second year running for the
two-part madrigal class at the
Herts Federation of Women's
Institutes' singing festival at
Welwyn Garden City on Saturday. The choir of only ten
was one of the smallest
competing.

The jubilant ladies are,
back row: Mrs. J. Blagg, Mrs.
E. Brown, Mrs. B. Wallace,
Mrs. S. Winter, Mrs. P.
Webster, Mrs. M. Innes, Mrs.
R. White. Front row, Mrs. M.
Coute, Mrs. E. Williamson,
Mrs. M. Whitby and Mrs. C.
Arthur.—RD8608.

spoke of the importance and necessity of saving and appealed to members to form a group of collectors to replace those now retiring. At the January 1947 meeting, Helpers in the Home scheme was discussed. The County Council were asking for helpers to go into homes where there were cases of illness; these helpers would be paid.

At the April meeting it was suggested holding a fete on August Bank Holiday. The Men's Club were to be asked to help and the fete would be held in the Bury Grounds. This was very successful and raised over £138 for the Village Hall Fund.

In May 1949 Mrs Legge, the chairman, said she was having tea with the Queen, who was opening the WI rally at Knebworth on 5 June. Two members were to be guards of honour, one of them to carry a placard with the name ASHWELL on it.

In March, Mrs Camp announced that Ashwell had 150 people over 60 to be catered for at the old folks' party. Petrol coupons had been received from the Fuel Office to help with the transport. There was to be quite a blow-out at the 1953 New Year's Party - 12 dozen bridge rolls, 4 loaves, 5 dozen sausage rolls, 6 quarts of milk, tin Nescafe. Half a pound of tea.

As the years progressed, the WI went from strength to strength. The Choir, founded in 1944, was successful in various competitions; and the remarkable range of activities, including that of its Drama Group, continued unabated.

In 1968, it celebrated its Golden Jubilee. Mrs Brookbanks, its President, planted two trees presented to Ashwell School to commemorate the Jubilee and a splendid dinner was held in November (12/6 a head) attended by over 80 members.

Members of Ashwell's WI took a keen interest in local and national affairs. They were often concerned at the litter- strewn streets, and so strong were their feelings in 1969 they cleaned up the High Street; in 1971 there was a sponsored rubbish round up in aid of the Village Garden Trust; and in April 1975 they were supporting a 'village clean-up'. Planning Applications, Pornography, the Health Services, traffic problems, were just a few of the many subjects covered.

This brief account, which cannot, due to space considerations, do proper justice to the work of the WI, should have laid to rest the "Jam and Jerusalem" myth which armchair critics have so mistakenly pontificated about. And if another Ashwell Book is published, its Diamond Jubilee in 1993 will be another milestone to celebrate its relevance to modern society.

The British Legion

The Ashwell Branch was formed in 1920/21 and in spite of ups and downs had kept going into the 90s, with about 60 members. In the 50s, 60s and 70s membership hovered around the 100 mark. In the 80s it was at times less than 50.

Much of the Legion's work has always been in the area of welfare, helping ex-service people when problems arise, particularly when they are the result of disablement due to war service.

Those who serve in a voluntary capacity tend to do so for lengthy periods. Philip Crump has served as Chairman from 1978 to the present: his father, Mark, was also Chairman until he died in 1965; members of the Crump family have been associated with the British Legion for 70 years! Robert Sheldrick has been Secretary since 1975. Another long serving Secretary was Stan Whitehead. Maurice Skinner has been Standard Bearer for 23 years, succeeding W Barton, who held the position for a long time. (Records available only go back to 1948.) Poppy Day has always been a vital event in British Legion activities, and its organiser for 32 years, until 1980, was Mrs J Revels. Edna Howes succeeded her in 1982. In 1952, the Poppy Day collection totalled over £65. In 1991 it was nearly £1200.

The regular activities of the Branch in Ashwell include an Annual Dinner, help with the parking arrangements at the August Bank Holiday Show, the Remembrance Sunday services, and distribution of Christmas vouchers to widows of ex- servicemen and others.

Finally, Mr Derrick Kingsley was Service Committee Secretary until 1991 having served since 1947.

The Village Hall

Soon after World War One a number of villages throughout the country considered the possibility of a central building where people could meet for public meetings, social occasions, dances, film shows, etc, in fact a village hall.

Some villages built war memorial halls but although some Ashwell people were of this opinion, it was not to be.

When Mrs Phyllis Fordham bought the old Page's Brewery at West End and offered to sell the malting for use as a village hall, some were still not in favour.

They pointed out that a village hall should be near the village centre, and that it should be a new, brick built structure, whereas the malting was not only built below ground level, which could result in damp problems, but the walls were built with the local clay bats (clay, chalk and straw, sun dried blocks) which could lead to great expense in the future. However, the scheme went ahead.

The malting was bought for £450 in 1922 and after a considerable amount of fundraising was renovated and equipped as a village hall, to be run by a Social Council, on which user organisations were represented. A stone tablet built into the clay bat wall states: 'Through the generosity and personal service of Mrs W A Fordham this building, originally a malting, was converted into a village hall and equipped as a centre for social life. "Till we have built Jerusalem in England's green and pleasant land".' The hall proved a great success. All the local organisations made use of it for dinners, dances, film shows, the Ashwell Choral and Dramatic Society, the Men's Social Club, Women's Institute, etc found it most useful. For small meetings the kitchen could be hired at a cheap rate; the kitchen also housed the Ashwell branch of the County library, and there was the great advantage of the two bathrooms where, for sixpence, any villager could take a bath by arrangement with the caretaker. It should be remembered that at that time there were very few bathrooms in Ashwell.

By 1939 the village hall was becoming a bit the worse for wear. There were ambitious plans to convert the old Page's Brewery itself into a Village Hall, to make it into a 'Keep Fit' centre, with swimming bath, dressing rooms, etc.

But the war put a stop to all that and anyway the Brewery was demolished in 1947. This made way for a garden for Westbury Cottage and parking space for visitors to the Village Hall.

In the meantime, the Village Hall had been used extensively during the war and for some years afterwards it was a popular venue. In the late 1950s, however, it was falling into a state of disrepair, the Social Council ceased to operate in 1960, and the Hall actually closed down. However, David Holbrook formed a Committee with the object of getting it into a fit state to run as a Youth Club. It re-opened in 1961, having obtained grants from the County Council. A new Trust was formed to lease the property from the original Trust, with Peter Howes as Secretary of a new Management Committee. Peter has, in succession to his father, a trustee in 1923, served the Village Hall cause right up to 1993.

Until 1973, the Youth Club flourished, first with a full time Leader, then Ted Worboys on a part-time basis but, with the latter becoming more involved in his business commitments, no new youth leader forthcoming and structural repairs to the building being necessary, matters came to a crisis point again. There were three choices: dispense with it, repair it, or build a new Hall and Community Centre. The debate also had the recent addition of the new Assembly Hall at Ashwell School to bear in mind.

Eventually, in 1974, the decision was taken - repair the Hall at the least possible expense. This happened, the Youth Club carried on there, further major improvements took place in the 80s and early 90s and probably now in 1993 the Village Hall is in as good a condition as it will ever be.

Ashwell at Rest (AS)

"The best preserved and most charming village near London", is a description applied to the Hertfordshire village of Ashwell by Sir Albert Richardson, when President of the Royal Academy.

Visitors are asked to spare a thought for the untold numbers of Ashwellians who have been buried in the churchyard since at least the twelfth century.

The first to be buried here in the original churchyard were rudely disturbed when early in the 14th century it was decided to build a new and larger church.

When the men digging the foundations unearthed the earlier Ashwellians, nice and snug in their stone coffins, the builders decided that the stone was far too valuable to bury again, so the coffins were built into the walls of the new church, where they can be seen today.

Before World War I ended (in which 45 of Ashwell's young men died) the church yard was filled. Charles Walkden, who came to Ashwell in the 1890s, thought it was overfilled then. In his book he tells of the day he watched a grave being dug and counted sufficient bones being thrown out by the sexton to form three skeletons. Towards the end of the war, a 'flu' epidemic swept through the country, and many died. Doctor Woodforde said that the German prisoners of war at the Maltings camp suffered badly. One prisoner, Julius Stamp, died and was the first to be buried in the new cemetery. I believe his remains were later taken to another cemetery. During the 1950s two animal bones were found by Cliff Bonnett when digging a grave in the cemetery. They were said to be about 2,000 years old.

As the country settled down after the World War I, memorial plans were drawn up all over the country. In London, the Cenotaph was designed by Sir Edwyn Lutyens; at Hinxworth, the little clock tower. At Ashwell, there were two main suggestions: a Portland stone cross designed by Sir Edwyn Lutyens or a gatehouse chapel at the entrance to the cemetery. Plans for both were drawn up, the winner was the stone cross. House-to-house collections were made and the cross bearing the names of the fallen was erected on a corner of the recreation ground and dedicated in 1922. After some years it was found necessary to build a cemetery chapel and this was designed by Sir Albert Richardson.

During the year 1948 I was asked by Brays (at that time undertakers as well as builders) to help with a funeral, as one of the regular bearers was ill. I was issued with a bowler hat, black jacket and striped trousers. Ashwell at that time owned a four-wheeled bier. With the coming of the crematoria at Cambridge and Luton, the bier, which in 1950 was about to collapse, was discarded and it became necessary to hire a motor hearse. This was owned and driven by a Letchworth builder and undertaker, Mr R W Smith, known to his friends as 'Rainwater Smith'. When Rainwater retired, the hearse was taken over by Cecil Lake. I soon found that work as a bearer must not be taken too seriously, though there were many sad occasions, such as when we buried Dick Gifford, a popular young married man who died of polio. There were times when we were held up whilst late arrivals wished to look at the deceased before the coffin lid was screwed down, there were cases when the dear departed swelled up and it was difficult to screw down the lid. Some of the cottages had difficult staircases, wicked words were said whilst the coffin was twisted and turned or even up-ended. One day a coffin got stuck half way down the grave, the grave had not been dug wide enough. We waited until the parson and mourners had departed, then up it came until the sides were made wider.

For some years one grave caused a good deal of interest; a small notice at one end bore three chromium letters - D A D - and facing it at the other end were the letter - M U M - suggesting that someone's Mum and Dad were sitting there looking at each other.

Bertie Ronald Brown and Albert Henry Brown lived with their wives and families side by side in Back Street. At the farm nearby lived their employer, Maurice Frederick Brown. Albert Henry Brown (always known as Geordie) died in 1980, aged 63, and was buried at the cemetery.

Bertie Ronald Brown died in 1981 and was buried at the cemetery. Shortly after the second interment, Geordie's widow paid a visit to her late husband's grave and was horrified to find that both men had been deposited in the same grave. To rectify this grave error, I understand that the grave digger was able to tunnel into the side of the grave and then gently slide Bertie over to his new resting place.

Occasionally we had a funeral away from Ashwell and on these occasions our old friend Cecil, the hearse driver, would draw on his wonderful collection of funeral anecdotes. At Norton churchyard he pointed out the gravestone of Polly Smith (mother of the great evangelist, Gipsy Smith) who died of smallpox in a tent nearby in 1865. For fear of infection the body was buried at night, without being taken into church, but in spite of these precautions not a single person attended church on the following Sunday. Inside Norton church, Cecil pointed out a most unusual monument to baby Anne, who was born the 12 September, 1652, and died 15 February 1652. The third daughter of Thomas Cole of Radwell Gent. and his wife Katherine.

Farmer, Frank Brown, of Dixies Farm, Ashwell, died in 1953, and according to his wishes he was taken to be buried at the Bedfordshire village of Stondon, where the rest of his family had been buried. On the return journey to Ashwell, Cecil suggested that we pull in at Henlow for a cup of tea. As we entered the cafe - the undertaker with his top hat, the rest of us in black suits and bowler hats - a taxi driver stopped drinking his tea and exclaimed, "Gor blimey, I thought he wasn't being buried till tomorrow". The funeral of King George VI was being held the next day!

When our old friend Cecil retired he was interviewed by the local press. The young reporter asked Cecil, "Mr Lake, what are your thoughts upon retirement?" Looking very serious, but with his usual dry humour, Cecil replied. "I am very sad. It's a dying trade'.

List of Subscribers

Bette Albon, 15 Bedford Road, Ickleford, Hitchin.

John and Doreen Anderson, 148 Miller Way, Brampton, Huntingdon, Cambs.

M/s Olive Anderson, 23 Kingsland Way, Ashwell, Herts.

Miss I.G. Badcock, 8 Wiggenhall Road, Watford, Herts.

Mrs Valerie Bagnall (nee McBeal), 1 Lower Farm House, Edworth.

Robin Barker, 38 Pryor Road, Baldock, Herts.

Sandra Barker, Swan Cottage, 6 Gardiners Lane, Ashwell, Herts.

Dorothy and George Berry, 24 Dixies Close, Ashwell, Herts.

David and Mary Billson, Elm Tree Cottage, Letchworth Lane, Letchworth, Herts.

Debbie and Colin Blumenau, 72 High Street, Ashwell, Herts.

Cliff and John Bonnett, 79 Station Road, Ashwell, Herts.

John and Avis Brockett, 50 Hay Street, Steeple Morden, Cambs.

Pauline and Peter Brook, Warren Lodge, 91 Back Street, Ashwell, Herts.

B. M. Browne, 39 Byde Street, Hertford, Herts.

Audrey and Harry Bullard, 81 Back Street, Ashwell, Herts.

Brian and Val Busby, 4 Woodforde Close, Ashwell, Herts.

Mike Buzzard, West End Cottage, Ashwell, Herts.

Anthony and Anita Catterick, 59 The Crescent, Abbots Langley, Herts.

Christopher and Carol Catterick, 9 Fouracre, Fenstanton, Cambs.

Judith E. Catterick, (widow of Canon Jack Catterick), Beckets, 20 Hodwell, Ashwell, Herts.

Maureen Catterick, (widow of the Rev. Peter Catterick), 2 Granhams Court, De Freville Road, Great Shelford, Cambridge.

Michael and Evelyn Catterick, 26 Fairfield Road, Aldeburgh, Suffolk.

Ian and Liz Chandler, Kirby Manor, High Street, Ashwell, Herts.

Mr D. H. Chapman, 301 Wedon Way, Bygrave, Herts.

Brian Cherry, 5 Sollershott West, Letchworth, Herts.

Mr and Mrs K Coiley, 8 Lucas Lane, Ashwell, Herts.

Graham and Susan Collins, 8 Nursery Close, Biggleswade, Beds.

Lindsay and Anne Colquhoun, Bear House, Ashwell, Herts.

Iain Colquhoun, Bear House, Ashwell, Herts.

Alison Colquhoun, Bear House, Ashwell, Herts.

Andrew and Pam(ela) Colquhoun, The Beeches, Wendover, Bucks.

Lachlan Colquhoun, Bear House, Ashwell, Herts.

May and Geoff Cook, 'Ashbrook', 10 Lucas Lane, Ashwell, Herts.

John and Marion Copperwheat (nee Gurney), Rothley House, Flitwick Road, Westoning, Beds.

Mavis and James Crabtree, Rhee House, Springhead, Ashwell, Herts.

Philip and Geraldine Crump, 15 Swan Street, Ashwell, Herts.

William J. Davies, 3 Fox Hill, Guilden Morden, Cambs.

Howard Day, 'Glendale', Brook End, Steeple Morden, Cambs.

Mr and Mrs P. Day, 76 Ashwell Street, Ashwell, Herts.

Ethel Dilley, 39 Wolverley House, Gardiners Lane, Ashwell, Herts.

Robin and Catherine Dunlop, Ashwell Grange, Ashwell, Herts.

Mr and Mrs G. Ellard, Armingford, 23 High Street, Guilden Morden, Cambs.

Norman and Jill Elliot, 12 Fox Hill Road, Guilden Morden, Cambs.

Mr H M. Evans, Coach House, 63 High Street, Ashwell, Herts.

Gill and Barry Field, 34 West End, Ashwell, Herts.

Brenda and Reg Fitzgerald, 'Westlands', 65 Station Road, Ashwell, Herts.

Roy and Liz Fitzsimmons, London House, High Street, Ashwell, Herts.

C. J. K. Fordham, Odsey Park, Ashwell, Herts.

Mrs J. Foster, 21 Silver Street, Ashwell, Herts.

Mrs Mavis Fox (nee McBeal), 76 Ashwell Street, Ashwell, Herts.

A. J. Francis, The Guild House, 55 High Street, Ashwell, Herts.

Marjorie Gentle, El Rancho, Hinxworth Road, Ashwell, Herts.

Mr and Mrs C. H. Godfrey, 43 West End, Ashwell, Herts.

Mrs H. G. Goodall, 11 Lucas Lane, Ashwell, Herts.

Sheila Graham, 2 Forresters Cottages, High Street, Ashwell, Herts.

Eric and Audrey Gurney, Ashridge Farm, Ashwell, Herts.

Joyce Gurney, 7 Eagle Drive, Flitwick, Beds.

Ron, Anne, Martin and Gemma Hancock, 51 Ashwell Street, Ashwell, Herts.

Peter Hankin, 66 Ashwell Street, Ashwell, Herts.

Keith William Hardyman, 7 Dynes Place, Moggerhanger, Beds.

Michael William Hardyman, 31 Nursery Close, Biggleswade, Beds.

David F. Harrowell, 30 Station Road, Arlesey, Beds.

Mary Haylock, Willian, Herts.

Dr and Mrs M. G. Hoffman, Chapel House, Hinxworth, Herts.

Mr John Hollings, 40 Woodriding Court, Dagmar Road, Wood Green, London.

Roy D. Holloway, 27 Back Street, Ashwell, Herts.

Mr and Mrs R. P. Howes, 54 Back Street, Ashwell, Herts.

Evelyn, David, Christopher and Andrew Hudson, 9 Eden Grove, Morpeth, Northumberland.

Gillian Grayling Humphreys, 'The Dormers', 19 Lucas Lane, Ashwell, Herts.

Brian and Janet Hunt, 3 Angells Meadow, Ashwell, Herts.

Mrs Gladys Ilett (nee Daniels), 14 Jubilee Way, Steeple Morden, Cambs.

Trevor and Chris James and Edward, 56 Back Street, Ashwell, Herts.

Mike Jeffes, 5 The Rickyard, Ashwell, Herts.

Vanessa and Cliff Jenkinson, 86 High Street, Ashwell, Herts.

Mrs Kathleen Jones (nee McBeal), 1 Lower Farmhouse, Edworth.

Mr and Mrs A. R. Kitely, Gatley End Farm, Steeple Morden, Cambs.

Mr and Mrs H. Krypczyk, Linda and Mark, Manor Farm, Hinxworth, Herts.

Mr and Mrs M. D. Leary, The School House, Odsey, nr Ashwell, Herts.

Rodney and Marilyn Leete, 53 Ashwell Street, Ashwell, Herts.

Robin and Eve Lipscombe, Hunt's Ridge, Ashwell Street, Ashwell, Herts.

Douglas and Betty Lockwood, 34 Station Road, Steeple Morden, Cambs.

Martin McBeal, 99 Station Road, Ashwell, Herts.

David and Susan Marsh, James, Christopher and Hannah, Springside Cottage, 2 High Street, Ashwell, Herts.

Andrew Martindale, Abbot's Hall Farm House, Aylsham, Norfolk.

Andrew Masson, 5 Willsheres Rd, Biggleswade, Beds.

I. J. Mitchell, 65 Northcott Avenue, Wood Green, London.

R. P. Mitchell, 1 New Road, Guilden Morden, Cambs.

Mr and Mrs T. J. Mitchell, 15 Wilbury Road, Letchworth, Herts.

Donald Keith Morris, 2 Pankhurst Crescent, Stevenage, Herts.

Jane, Nicholas and Sara Moss, The Old Cottage, High Street, Ashwell, Herts.

Dr and Mrs F. D. Moynihan, Pope's Farm, Ashwell, Herts.

Raymond and Angela Munday, 53 High Street, Ashwell, Herts.

Richard and Cicely Murfitt, 14 Silver Street, Guilden Morden, Cambs.

Vic and Vera Olley, Digswell Manor, High Street, Ashwell, Herts.

A. Oyston, 3 Buttway, Ashwell, Herts.

Patrick Oyston, Mobbs Hole Farm, Northfield Road, Ashwell, Herts.

Ruth and Reg Papworth, 10 Common Road, Stotfold, Beds.

Mrs Wendy Penn (nee Collins), Bassingbourn, Cambs.

The Rev. and Mrs Frank Pickard, 58 Angerstien Close, Weeting, Norfolk.

Guy and Karen Pickett, R.A.F.

John and Jane Pickett, 8 Peacocks Close, Cavendish, Suffolk.

Leo and Christine Pickett, 'Chakrata', 3 Newnham Way, Ashwell, Herts.

Alan Picking, 17 West End, Ashwell, Herts.

Leon F. Picking, 120 Guants Way, Letchworth, Herts.

Clare Pollard, 12 Roselea, Impington, Cambridge.

Mr and Mrs W. J. A. Porteous, 73 Back Street, Ashwell, Herts.

Mr A. G. Potter and L. A. Potter, 408 Main Road, Coromandell Valley, South Australia, 5051.

Andrew J. Pye, 39 Station Road, Steeple Morden, Cambs.

Mrs N. M. Reeves, 9 Lucas Lane, Ashwell, Herts.

Carys, David, Anna and Katharine Roberts, Bronant, High Street, Ashwell, Herts.

Sheila Rosendale, 5 Green Road, Newnham, Herts.

John and Gaye Rowlands, Jonathan, Mark and Matthew, The Elms, Lucas Lane, Ashwell, Herts.

Sue and Dai Rowley Jones, Worlands, Ashwell Street, Ashwell, Herts.

Byron and Fay Searle, 18 Dixies Close, Ashwell, Herts.

Mary and Derek Sells, 27 Courtlands Drive, Biggleswade, Beds.

John M. Sheldrick, Middle Farm, Hinxworth, Herts.

N. J. Sheldrick, 107 Southfields, Letchworth, Herts.

Robert J. Sheldrick, 29 Mill Street, Ashwell, Herts.

Gurney Sheppard, Ashwell Bury, Ashwell, Herts.

Jonathon Sheppard, Ashwell Bury, Ashwell, Herts.

Diana and Peter Shuttlewood, 21 Sunnymead Orchard, Station Road, Ashwell, Herts.

The Simmons Family, 68 Ashwell Street, Ashwell, Herts.

Mrs Elizabeth Stone, 18 Woodforde Close, Ashwell, Herts.

Robert and Corrie Swain, 32 Hodwell, Ashwell, Herts.

Mr I and Mrs J. M. Thomas, Next Odsey, Station Road, Ashwell, Herts.

Lesley and Nicholas Tracey-Williams, Farrowby Farm, Hinxworth, Herts.

Margaret Waide, 49 High Street, Ashwell, Herts.

Mrs Bessie Wallace, Sale's Acre, Ashwell, Herts.

David and Rachel Walton (nee Gurney) , 8 Tasman Road, Haverhill, Suffolk.

David Ward, 17 Britannia Avenue, Whitstable, Kent.

J. L. Watts, 463 Glenfield Road, Glenfield, Auckland, New Zealand.

A. P. Westcott (mother nee Chalkley), 29a Benslow Rise, Hitchin, Herts.

Alan and Rosemary White, 93 Station Road, Ashwell, Herts.

Aileen and Aubrey Wright, 99 Hay Street, Steeple Morden, Cambs.